YOU need to stop complaining, pointing fingers, passing the buck, and making excuses so you can finally make every sale.

P.S. Don't make me repeat myself.
P.P.S. Always have a "P.S."
P.P.P.S. It's "P.P.S.", not "P.S.S." Learn how to communicate for heaven's sake. It's your job as a salesperson. Now start reading, applying, growing, and making every sale.

.ₐₛ$$$$$$$$$$$$$$$$$$$ₛₛₛₐ

"IF YOU'RE LOOKING FOR INSPIRATION AND ARE TIRED OF THE GOO-ROOS AND THE CLOSERS AND YOU'VE GOT YOUR CHAKRA AND YOUR CHI IN ALIGNMENT WITH YOUR FENG SUI AND YOUR TAZO CHAI TEA LATTE AND YOU HAVE A FEW DOLLARS TO SPARE** AND THEY HAVE THE BOOK IN STOCK THEN THAT MEANS IT'S AVAILABLE THEN THIS JUST MIGHT, MAYBE BE THE BOOK FOR YOU."***

* I know this isn't a motto that just rolls off the tongue but it's how you probably—and your prospects most definitely—are thinking, and it's our job as sales professionals to meet our prospects where they are.

** If spending a few bucks on a book causes you angst and consternation…you really need this book, _so buy it_, read it, and engage in my free group at **TheImplementors.com**. It's time you made some money and learning how to sell"The Sales Whisperer® Way" is the best thing you can do for your wallet.

*** If you're not into reading and just want to get down to business, go to **TheSalesWhisperer.com/ipa** and let's get to work.

.»$$$$$$$$$$$$$$$$$$$$s.

"One Word - PROFOUND. This book has done more than you know for me
right now."
~Omari Broussard, Owner, 10X Defense

P.S. There ain't too much whisperin'
goin' on up in here.

Wes Schaeffer

..ₛₛ$$$$$$$$$$$$$$$$$$$ₛₛₛₛₛₛ

ALSO BY WES SCHAEFFER

The Definitive Guide To Infusionsoft: How Mere Mortals Increase Traffic, Leads, Prospects, Sales, Testimonials, Online Orders & Referrals With the World's Most Powerful Small Business Sales & Marketing Automation Software

The Sales Whisperer® Press Publisher
Cover design: Wes Schaeffer
Composition and production: TSW Group, Inc.

This publication is designed to provide accurate and
authoritative information in regard to the subject matter
covered. It is sold with the understanding that the publisher
is not engaged in rendering legal, accounting, or other
professional services. If legal advice or other expert
assistance is required, the services of a competent
professional person should be sought.

ISBN: 978-0-9858311-2-7
1.Selling. 2. Marketing. 3. Advertising. I. Schaeffer, Wes

Printed in the United States of America

Sales, Business, Jiu-Jitsu, & Life

Everyone gets into jiu-jitsu out of genuine interest. Face it, you have to be a certain type of person to let someone who is trying to hurt you get that close.

But there seems to be a certain number of individuals that think the journey is easy and every moment will be filled with joy.

——— IT'S NOT. ———

For the first year or so you will make a lot of mistakes, you won't be good.
You will come to every class, you will have a lot of potential, but nothing will click.

Everything you did before, all your accomplishments, forget them.
They will not keep you from getting smashed.

A lot of people never get past this stage, they quit.

In fact, most people don't have a hard year, they have a hard few.

We know we have some missing links, but we are one step away from a major breakthrough....We just don't know the solution.

EVERYONE GOES THROUGH THIS.

And if you are just starting out or you are still in this stage,
you have to realize it's normal and all you have to do is

PUT IN MORE TIME ON THE MATS.

Be the first to arrive, last to leave.

Doesn't matter if you have to **tap a little more**, cry alittle harder, drill a little longer.

It's only by putting in sustained and focused effort what you will begin **to reach the next level.**

The result of this will be technique as good as those who came before you

and the medals on your wall will clink every time you shut the door
and your belt will look older than you.

It's going to take a while, that's normal.

You just have to roll through the hardships,
and sometimes push through the pain.

The picture on the previous page is of a poster on the wall at the Brazilian Jiu-Jitsu school at which I've trained since January 2017.

Replace the word "jiu-jitsu" with entrepreneurship or business or sales or parenthood or marriage and re-read it.

"Everyone gets into jiu-jitsu out of genuine interest."

You probably thought it would be fun or exciting or liberating or easy to get into sales, to launch a business, to marry the man or woman of your dreams.

"Face it, you have to be a certain type of person to let someone who is trying to hurt you get that close."

Now I hope your spouse is not trying to hurt you physically but anytime you open your heart you are vulnerable to being hurt and when it comes to business, which is nothing without sales, your prospects don't care if you stay open or not as long as they get a great price from you. So are you ready for that kind of crazy?

"But there seems to be a certain number of individuals that think the journey is EASY and every moment will be filled with joy."

You see people looking for the easy button every hour of every day. They think that because they care and because they use organic ingredients and because they donate to PETA or drive a Prius their customers will love them, their staff will love them, and they'll never have a single argument at home, and their kids will eat their vegetables and brush their teeth without asking.

"IT'S NOT."

I'm sorry if you were looking for a trigger warning but there are no safe spaces on the Brazilian Jiu-Jitsu mat, in this book, or in real life, upon which this book is based. But at least I didn't sneak up on you. I opened with this message of tough love. Can you handle it? Good, because it gets better…and it will help you in every area of your life.

"For the first year or so you will make a lot of mistakes, you won't be good."

When you learned to walk, feed yourself, ride a bike, roller-skate, hit a golfball, play the piano...you were bad. But anything worth doing is worth doing poorly until you get good at it. This applies to your relationships, your career, and the business you want to launch.

"You will come to every class, you will have a lot of potential, but nothing will click."

You will buy courses and books, attend conferences and read blogs, hire staff and consultants, join expensive masterminds and waste time and money on social media and paid ads, but nothing will work.

"Everything you did before, all your accomplishments, forget them. They will not keep you from getting smashed."

Oh, you were Prom King in high school and you think that means something to your wife that you didn't meet until two years after college? Oh, you won the 8th grade science fair so you think your prospects shouldn't question the ingredients in your new green shake mix? Oh, you won the hotdog eating contest at your fraternity all eights years of undergrad on your daddy's dime so you think you should be promoted to sales manager the first time you actually make quota one quarter? Get a life...and get ready to get punched in the nose.

"A lot of people never get past this stage, they quit."

People quit marriages after months or even weeks. They bounce from job to job after a year or less. They raise money for the greatest idea ever, only to close their doors and leave town in the dead of night. And I can't count how many people have signed up for Jiu-Jitsu and quit after their first week, first month, or within days of getting their blue belt.

"In fact, most people don't have a hard year. They have a hard few."

That's life. Nothing worth doing is ever easy but we believe what we see on TV and think we can solve world hunger and earn a gold medal in 43 minutes. People aren't just sitting by the phone with their credit cards in their hands waiting for you to call them. And whatever tool, technology, or tactic you used to reach them last year is barely working this year and won't work at all next year. So stay on top of your game, continue to practice, drill, rehearse, evolve, test, measure, adapt, and overcome.

"We know we have some missing links, but we are one step away from a major breakthrough…we just don't know the solution."

How many times have you seen—and even shared—the Edison quote "I have not failed. I've just found 10,000 ways that won't work"? Isn't that inspiring? Isn't that motivating? Isn't that nostalgic? Isn't it also mostly crap? I mean, sure, it's true and he probably said it and he probably believed it. But he was a unique individual who was well-funded and had a friggin' army of scientists and staff working for him and developing other projects that lined his pockets quite nicely. When you have a wife, an 11-month old son, and you're on unemployment when your second son is born, you're ready to go work at the Post Office by the second or third failure and I guarantee you that you don't have the runway for 10,000 tries.

"EVERYONE GOES THROUGH THIS."

Hi my little snowflake. Yes, you are special and unique…just like everyone else.

"And if you are just starting out or you are still in this stage, you have to realize it's normal and all you have to do is PUT IN MORE TIME ON THE MATS."

The problems you face—divorce, drug/alcohol abuse, bankruptcy, foreclosure, repossession, failed businesses, infidelity, lawsuits, DUI, miscarriages, all of the above—have been faced and overcome by millions of people and are being handled with aplomb so suck it up, wipe away your tears, and get back to getting after it. Write more ads, create more blog posts, send more emails, attend more trade shows, make more cold calls, send more direct mail, modify your product offerings.

"Be the first to arrive, last to leave."

Pour more gas on the fire, make another pot of coffee, show up 30 minutes earlier, stay 30 minutes longer, hire another coach, invest in another program, just keep going.

"Doesn't matter if you have to tap a little more, cry a little harder, drill a little longer."

Yes, sometimes you will want to cry. Sometimes you will cry. Some days things will click, but many days you will discover 100 ways to NOT succeed. All you will do is tap out from sunrise to sunset.

"It's only by putting in sustained and focused effort that you will begin to reach the next level."

Each time your idea fails it is instructive but you must keep an open mind to see, understand, and recognize how to apply that lesson to your next effort.

"The result of this will be technique as good as those who came before you and the medals on your wall will clink every time you shut the door and your belt will look older than you."

The "C" students hire the "B" students to manage the "A" students. Mark Cuban, Jeff Bezos, Martha Stewart, Oprah are not from another planet. They're not divine beings. They were just focused and tenacious. How driven are you? (If you've checked your email or social media accounts in the three minutes it has taken to read this I'd say you're not very focused, driven, or committed. But at least you know now and if you can measure it, you can improve it.)

"It's going to take a while. That's normal. You just have to roll through the hardships, and sometimes push through the pain."

As I write this both of my knees hurt that require an extra 20 minutes of stretching and warmups to train, my right hand knuckle at the base of my pinkie has been jammed for 8 days so I've been essentially fighting with one hand for a week and it'll probably be another week before it's healed, and both elbows have knots in them from gripping so I can't push off a heavy opponent easily. Oh yeah, my ribcage is also sore, which makes me less able to withstand the pressure of even a smaller opponent.

But you know what I'll do today, for the fifth time this week? Train Brazilian Jiu-Jitsu for at least 90 minutes. Maybe two hours. But only after waking up at 5 AM on a Saturday to write for three hours.

Yes, I'd like a little more sleep. Yes, I'd like my body to not be battered and bruised. Yes, I'd like my business to grow faster, my belly to grow slower, and my kids to grow slower still.

But I'm willing to do what it takes for as long as it takes to get where I want to be in all areas of my life. My goal is to help you do the same with this book and the programs and consulting I offer.

Now go sell something! 👍

$ssssss$$$$$$$$$$$$$$ssss

Dedication

*This book is dedicated to anyone that has ever
entered the winner-take-all arena of sales
armed with little more than an idea, a work ethic,
and a "whatever-it-takes" attitude.
Where there are no safety nets, no do-overs,
and no timeouts.
You lived to sell another day and because of
your sales efforts,
your clients, your company, your
family, and you are better off.*

Now go sell something!

.ₐₛ$$$$$$$$$$$$$$$$$$$$$$$ₛₛₛₛ

Acknowledgments

Thank you to my momma, Debbie, for ~~proof-reading~~ ~~proofreeding~~ reviewing this book (But not this section. I snuck it in after she was done.) and for giving me a good brain. I mean, I really have a very good brain, and I've said and written a lot of things. I probably have the greatest brain. I'm really smart. I talk to myself and consult myself on all things pertaining to business and I give myself really great advice thanks to the brain my momma gave me.

Thank you, as always, to my wife of 23 years, Shannon, for allowing me to sneak off to my office to work while she kept our 7 children fed, clothed, bathed, "homeworked," "soccered," "volleyballed," and entertained. She has the two hardest jobs in the world: wife of an entrepreneur and being a mom.

A Few Success Stories

"Our retainers have increased from between $175k-$200k per month to $250,000 per month within 90 days thanks to your training."

Zach Smith, President
Funded Today, #27 on Inc 500

"I just wanted to thank you for your suggestion that I (we) use an agenda for our prospect meetings. I have had three since I started using the agenda I adapted from yours. Both went MUCH better. One was a more narrowly focused meeting, which they let me know via email before our meeting. They were very impressed by the agenda AND we had a more focused meeting right from the start. So far, one has signed and the other two have give favorable verbal indications. One will receive my proposal package tomorrow and the other will receive theirs on Friday which enables them to discuss it with their sons over the weekend.

"Thank you and God bless you!"

Katherine O'Brien
Celtic College Consultants

"Wes, you showed me how to grow my leads 383% in our first month, 337% the second month, raise my prices 2x-10x, and grow my paid subscribers 54% all within 90 days."

Alycia Wicker
www.AlyciaWicker.com

"Dude, you were born to sell!"

Landon Ray
Founder & CEO, Ontraport

Contents

.₁s$$$$$$$$$$$$$$$$$ₛₛₛ.

Foreword
By TeeJ Mercer

I hate writing! I really do. Four books later, I still hate writing! Yet, here we are.

I apologize if my bold declaration offends your senses but if you knew me, then you would know I always tell you the truth and I will always be transparent.

Which leads me to my next point…

Since you are reading this, then it's safe to assume my love for Wes Schaeffer overrode my desire to watch paint dry instead of writing a foreword for him.

LawdHamMussyGeezus! OMG! I hate that he will read the nice things I write.

I hate that I have to tell the truth and tell y'all what I really think of Wes because now his head is only going to get bigger than it already is, and he'll forever give me grief about it.

But no doubt, Wes Schaeffer changed the game for me. It's just that simple.

At the beginning of what I call my "reluctant entrepreneur" journey, Wes was my Infusionsoft consultant so I landed on his email list.

Not only did he dispense his valuable genius, just like he does within these pages but he also did it in an in-your-face but totally implementable manor. The cherry on top was that his messages were seasoned with his unapologetic Christian faith.

For me…that works! I was smitten with his genius and fortunately his wife was okay with it.

You see, I'm a 20+ year Hollywood veteran with big TV shows under my belt. I now use that expertise to show folks how to book their own media and rock their genius on media outlets around the country like ABC, CBS, FOX, NBC and more.

Before Wes, not only did I not know how to assign a dollar figure to my expertise but I also didn't know how to position myself so that potential clients could see the value in partnering with my genius so I could help them blow their business, book, or brand in the media.

But babyyyyyyyy…

When "The Sales Whisperer" added his practical, ethical strategy magic to my unicorn sparkle, my business, Media Mavericks Academy took off.

Wes' approach to sales is just what I needed—solid, tested strategies infused with heart and comedy.

I can't tell you the number of times I've gone to Wes with a question and walked away with a complete strategy THAT WORKED!

As you journey through the plethora of delicious insightful yummy nuggets that Wes drops along *The Sales Whisperer Way*, I am certain you will relate, connect, embrace and eventually transform your thinking about sales.

I sure have.

Although I know I'm not his only client, I sure do feel like it. The time, concern, and follow-up he provides is like a big brother picking on you and looking out for you at the same time.

Don't tell him, but I can't imagine not having Wes' steady hand guiding me along this entrepreneur journey. By the time you read the last word, you'll want to get some Wes in your life too.

Now, turn the page so Wes can show you how to "Go sell something!"

TeeJ Mercer
Chief NoiseMaker, Media Mavericks Academy
MediaMavericks.tv

Introduction

On September 1, 2006 I was watching "The Dog Whisperer" and heard Cesar Millan's tagline, "I rehabilitate dogs and train their owners." I sat up in my chair and thought, "That's what I do except I 'rehabilitate sales people and train their managers." I remember the date because I immediately logged into GoDaddy and bought the domain name, TheSalesWhisperer.com. Not 10 days later I was contacted by someone to buy the name from me. (I'm sure glad I said no.)

At the time, I was about a year into building the foundation for The Sales Whisperer®. I knew what I wanted it to be and I knew I would get there, but I wasn't exactly sure how.

That's what makes sales people such a fundamental part of any economy. We have the faith, the courage, the optimism, (the madness?), to leave our homes and venture into the unknown to make a sale so our company can keep its doors open, employees and vendors paid and our families fed.

Now I have the confidence — and the time — to jot a few ideas on paper. This started as a compilation of my newsletter / musings I call The Weekly Whisper (you can subscribe for free at **WeeklyWhisper.com**).

But for now, enjoy this compilation of my best ideas as put forth between 2007 and 2018 in The Weekly Whisper. When you see concepts and ideas mentioned repeatedly, it means they are important, which is why I repeat them. Think of it as my way of stomping my foot at the front of the classroom and saying "this WILL be on the test." The test of business success.

Now go sell something! ~✲~

Take a Leap of Faith

In the Summer of 1997 I had it all:

- Two degrees from two great colleges.
- No college debt.
- A wife that loved me.
- A newborn son.
- Another son on the way (but we didn't know it, yet.)
- A three bedroom house on a golf course with a view of the bay.
- My house payment and bills were paid for.
- We had 100% medical coverage for my entire family for free.
- I lived five minutes from my office.
- We had every other Friday off.
- The golf club membership was $400 per year.
- My retirement pay was guaranteed.
- An annual raise was guaranteed.

In September 1997 I left it all behind to move into a 2-bedroom upstairs apartment, to a city where the only people I knew were my dad and stepmom to take a commissioned sales job with a stipend that didn't cover my bills and decreased every month. Hello turmoil, chaos, uncertainty, rejection, bottom of the totem pole, and the foundation of my future sales success.

"Leaving it all behind" is not for everyone, but I knew if we got much more "settled in" to the Air Force officer career, it would be too hard to leave. Deep down, I knew I was a bit of a rebel. I wanted to be paid for my production and effort, not for just time on the job.

It paid off. But it was not easy. It has been a bumpy road. I am still learning and growing and experimenting but I'm doing it on my own schedule, with the people and partners of my choosing and I'm doing it my way on my own terms, working from home, in shorts and flip flops, and I wouldn't have it any other way.

Listen to your little voices. Follow your gut. Be bold. Make your move and always remember that failure is an event, not a person, and until you fail, you won't know your limits. Ready to jump in? ~*~

P.S. 23 years later, I'd say the jump was worth it. Wouldn't you? I know Tabitha thinks so…

> *"Before I even got home, I did what you taught. As a result, I have doubled my membership numbers…did $3,200 in my first webinar…This put a fresh wind in my business…."* (Cont'd)
>
> *"I raised prices on my planner (423%) and it's now my best-selling product. You gave a backbone to this spineless work at home mom. Seriously! YOU ROCK!"*
>
> **Tabitha Day Philen**

I Believe

Here's what I believe:

- I believe in helping professional salespeople, sales managers, business owners and entrepreneurs find the exact tools and programs they need to grow, hence **www.BestCRMForMe.com**.
- I believe your time is valuable.
- I believe low quality solutions are never a good value.
- I believe quick fixes are quick for a reason.
- I believe in giving you back your money when something's not right and we can't fix it.
- I believe business is more fun when your tools are running fast, smooth, and making you money.
- I believe you don't have to be a pushy, sleazy jerk to make a lot of money in sales.
- I believe you have an inner child that wants to make people smile.
- I believe that making deep human connections is good for you.
- I believe in camp fires and sipping whiskey.
- I believe you'd be happier if you stared out the window more.
- I believe in delivering a powerful message in a powerful manner.
- I believe anyone can be great at generating inbound sales, even you.

And I believe you were born to grow.

Here's what I also believe:
- Capitalism provides the greatest path to prosperity.
- A so-called "open-minded/tolerant" person will stop reading this book maybe halfway down this page.
- Entrepreneurs are what make this country great.
- Bacon is the candy of meats.
- A business owner owes it to himself, his staff, his vendors, his family, and his clients to make as much money as possible by meeting their needs with excellence to ensure he stays in business.
- Children are a blessing from God.
- A business owner's #1 job is to market.
- The #1 goal of marketing is to build a big list.
- The #1 sin of marketing is being boring.
- A sales manager's #1 job is to recruit.
- A sales person's #1 job is to prospect.
- Entrepreneurs need more help **Implementing** and being held **Accountable** than generating ideas to really grow.

- The teaching/training methods and methodologies that sprung forth from the Industrial Revolution are not only inadequate and insufficient for success and happiness in 2019 and beyond, but are actually harmful and hindering our abilities to reach our full potential as citizens and entrepreneurs today.
- The lottery is for people who are bad with math.
- Political correctness is making America weak.
- People that feel "entitled" are making America weak.
- People who need "safe spaces" are making America weak.
- People who get "triggered" are making America weak.
- Businesses can only grow through dedicated, focused, hard work over an extended period of time.
- The SEC is the greatest college football conference in the universe. (Florida State got lucky...but their players are all SEC neighbors.)
- 99.9% of those who participate in social media marketing are not social, know nothing about media, and even less about marketing, which is why they (you?) fail.
- Cold calling still works and never stopped working.
- Only idiots and fools make old school, blind cold calls today.
- There is no one "right way" to grow your business.
- Marketing is just selling in print. To be a better marketer, learn how to sell.
- Yellow Pages can still get you clients (especially if you sell to Baby Boomers).
- Newspaper advertising can still get you clients.
- Radio advertising can still get you clients.
- TV advertising can still get you clients.
- Fax broadcasts can still get you clients. (And big fines, so do it right.)
- SEO still matters.
- Content is still king.
- Relevant content is the queen (but we know she tells the king how to dress, what to eat and when to STHU.)
- Text messaging can still get you clients. (And more big fines, so do it right.)
- Gary Halbert was right: Motion beats meditation.
- There is no problem you are facing now in your business that a 100% increase in profits can't fix.
- When you double your profits, you won't be problem-free. You'll just have a new set of problems.
- Handwritten notes/cards/letters can still get you clients.
- Phone calls can still get you clients.
- People that are easily-offended are not happy people and should be fired as clients.
- The only thing the government is good at is killing people and breaking things.
- You cannot tax your way into prosperity.

- Guns don't kill people.
- It's the drunk driver's fault and his fault alone.
- It's a life, not a choice.
- If you can measure it you can improve it.
- Two heads are better than one.
- You can't steer a parked car, so get moving. (See Gary Halbert above.)
- You can't read the label from inside the bottle.
- In the land of the blind, the one-eyed man is king. (See "How To Keep The Monsters Away" blog post.)
- History does repeat itself.
- Those that don't know history...are probably victims of public school education. (See the government killing people and breaking things.)
- Kids don't know better. Tell them what to eat, when to go to sleep, and what to watch on TV. Make them go to church with you on Sunday until they are 18, out of the house, and paying 100% of their own living and educational expenses, including their own health insurance and cell phone bill.
- We all need someone to look up to.
- I did build that.
- Healthcare is not a Constitutional right, nor should it be.
- Healthcare would be more affordable if the government got out of it.
- We don't have healthcare in America. We have "sickcare" and it's scary.
- We are eating ourselves to death in America.
- Mass media in America is no longer seeking the truth but is promoting an agenda.
- The worshipping of professional athletes is ridiculous.
- The "spiritual but not religious" are just too lazy to develop their consciences and their faith…get up and go to church on Sunday.
- God is love, and love is visible in our children and in our works. Since love is only present when there is someone else to love I believe in the Trinity.
- Shortcuts may produce short term results but always produce long term weaknesses.
- Your website is the hub—the center—of your marketing.
- In negotiating from a position of strength.
- Your company doesn't owe you anything.
- Unions have been ruined by greedy union bosses, which has lead to their demise.
- In Single Malt Scotch…
- And Blended Scotch…
- And bourbon…
- And cold beer in a frosty mug…
- And big Malbecs…
- And bigger cigars…
- And PING® putters…

- And carrying at least four wedges in your golf bag.
- That a crawfish boil is the best way to "pass a good time, cher."
- That the first person to eat an oyster was really hungry.
- Cold calling scripts work.
- Sales scripts work.
- Business can and does get done on the golf course.
- People will read long blog posts.
- People will read what interests them. Even ads. (Thanks Howard Luck Gossage.)
- The Earth does not need saving. (It's a 12,756.3 km around rock that weighs 5.972^24 kilograms. You and I need saving.)
- Multi-tasking is the art of doing two things half as well as they should be done.
- Implementing multi-media, multi-step nurture / follow-up sequences is the only way to grow your business.
- If you don't piss someone off by noon, you're not marketing. (Thanks, Dan Kennedy.)
- If you don't toot your own horn your competitors sure as hell won't.
- Your Mom was wrong. You need to talk to strangers to grow your business and make every sale. (**MakeEverySale.com**)
- Video is a great way to market your business.
- A smartphone makes video that is "good enough" to market your business. (See "steering parked cars" above.)
- Testimonials are great for marketing your business.
- Too few people ask for testimonials.
- Too few people ask for video testimonials.
- Referrals are great for growing your business.
- Too few people ask for referrals.
- Podcasts are a great way to market your business.
  - Subscribe to TheSalesPodcast.com
  - Subscribe to CRMSushiPodcast.com
- You won't get rich and famous by having a podcast.
- Email newsletters are a great way to market your business.
- Without Goliath, David would've died an unknown shepherd boy.
- ~~Typoes~~ Errors will always be found after you hit Send/Print/ Publish. Hit it anyway.
- In you, even if you…
  - Vote *differently* than me.
  - Have sex differently than me.
  - Get upset because I mentioned sex.
  - Practice your faith or spirituality or "religiousity" different than me.
  - Make more money than me.
  - Make less money than me.
  - Are single, divorced, or a newlywed.
  - Are taller than me.
  - Stronger than me.

- Shorter than me.
- Better at Brazilian Jiu-Jitsu than me.
- Dropped out of high school.
- Dropped out of college.
- Lost your home to foreclosure.
- Filed for bankruptcy.
- Are an alcoholic or addicted to pain medications or porn or shopping or hoarding or sex (I said it again...twice really because I think porn is related to sex) or gambling or you name it.

- I believe in you because I know that as long as you have air in your lungs and dreams and aspirations and even hopes and fears that you are still a work in progress and it ain't over 'til it's over.
- I believe, as Zig Ziglar always said, that failure is not a person, it's an event, and you cannot enjoy the fruits of your labor without a struggle. Without great effort.
- By the way, being handed fame and fortune because of great lips or hips or the fact you can dunk a basketball or parrot a line is why so many celebrities and athletes and rich kids end up a mess.
- God has us go through the birth canal for a reason. It's true the day you were born to the day you give birth to your business. So keep on keeping on.
- Don't sweat the petty things. (Pet the sweaty things?)
- Laugh more. Eat more fiber. Floss more often.
- Call your loved ones regularly.

What do you believe? ~✲~

You just gotta believe.

FromTodaysReading.com

Make Every Sale

When I say that in order to make ANY sale you must make EVERY sale, here's a case in point.

I get 5-10 pitches a day from PR firms who want me to interview their client on The Sales Podcast.

When I see a personal message it gets my attention and it makes an impression.

This email started off fine but then I see "Sales Podcast, The."

> Wes,
>
> I have a story I think Sales Podcast, The would want to cover.

I knew immediately that this was a blast sent with merge fields and they did a poor job of editing their CSV file when uploading to their marketing automation tool.

I scrolled to the bottom, found the Unsubscribe, and just like that I'm no longer a lead for them.

Could they look me up and mail me a letter or call me?

Sure.

But when someone is too lazy to edit their data upload, 999 times out of 1,000 they are too cheap and lazy to mail me a letter or call me.

To make any sale you must make every sale.

Now go sell something. ~✻~

Determination

"War is an ugly thing, but not the ugliest of things. The decayed and degraded state of moral and patriotic feeling which thinks that nothing is worth war is much worse. The person who has nothing for which he is willing to fight, nothing which is more important than his own personal safety, is a miserable creature and has no chance of being free unless made and kept so by the exertions of better men than himself."
~ **John Stuart Mill**

John was not a soldier. He was a philosopher.

This letter is not about war. It's about entrepreneurship.

I lead off with this quote because it is my all time favorite from college.

Where did I learn such a quote? In the foothills of the Rockies at the Air Force Academy during the summer of 1988. Freshmen had to memorize and deliver on demand all of the quotes and facts in this little booklet called "Contrails" at any time and any place that any upperclassman asked us to. After all these years, it still resonates in my mind and in my soul.

Today, we are at war literally and economically. (Buy me a beer and I'll tell you what I think of the shooting war. Keep reading and I'll tell you how to thrive during the fiscal war.) When I moved to SoCal in December of 2004, everyone from friends to family to the waitress at Denny's was telling me to buy real estate. "It's California real estate! You can't go wrong! It's growing to the moon. This time it's DIFFERENT! No money down. No-doc, interest-only loans. Just get in and get rich!!!"

I nodded. I smiled. I congratulated them on their wisdom and pending riches. Then I rented.

Fast forward to 2009:

- The market dropped 60% in my little Temecula Valley.
- The last Chamber of Commerce mixer could have been held in my garage.
- Empty car dealer lots collect tumbleweeds and graffiti.
- And I kept renting.
- And people I warned scratched their heads and looked at me differently (and it's not because of my cowboy boots in California.)

Yes, that's me in the newspaper on the other page and that's me in the middle with "The Chums." We're all still friends to this day

Was I lucky? Nope.
Was I informed? Yep.
Was my timing perfect? Nope.
Was it close enough to save $450,000? Yep.
Did I sometimes question my decision when my neighbors were living large? Yep.
Are my neighbors now gone, leaving behind green pools and brown yards? Oh yeah.

The Language of The Markets

Markets have languages that can be read and understood after great study and pondering and discussions amongst and between fellow ponderers. Would you like to know what my fellow ponderers see happening now? Would you like to be able to hear the language of the markets tomorrow so you can build your business bigger, better and more bullet-proof to scoop up the countless opportunities that always exist?
You and I know the world is:

A) Not comprised of better people than ourselves, and,
B) Not going to just roll over and hand us the future we know we deserve.

So say goodbye to easy money and stop seeking it.
Acknowledge you have something worth fighting for, which is our personal and entrepreneurial and financial freedom.
Get to work.
Harder than before, but with a clearer vision.
With focused steps.
With the support of your crazy, optimistic peers.
With the guidance of experts in sales, marketing, business.
I'll do my *bestest* to be that expert peer as you read on.

Be prepared to be called nuts, irrational, unrealistic, maybe even bat-shit crazy.

Welcome to the club. ~*~

Life's Too Short For Follow-Up Calls

Since 2006 I've been working on my USP—Unique Selling Proposition. In a nutshell, it's part tag line, part mission statement, part elevator pitch all rolled up into something short and sweet, pithy, memorable and impactful.

And like anything in life, good ones are hard to create. Then, around 2008, this tagline / USP came to me and it not only resonated with me but with other sales professionals, sales managers, business owners and entrepreneurs I knew. It resonated because we've all seen our Outlook calendars full of Tasks or self-set "Appointments" to "follow-up" with some prospect that has blown us off. Those amorphous, ambiguous, one-sided appointments just waste our time, the prospect's time and wear us down.

"But, Wes, follow-ups are important. I read that we need to have 7-12 touches or follow-ups with a prospect before they buy but now you're saying I shouldn't follow-up. WTH? Are you crazy? I need a drink."

You're right. It does take more touches to win over a prospect, but if you have a mutually-agreed upon date to get back in touch, you are not "following-up," you are calling in or arriving for your set "appointment."

Sure, some say it's semantics and I'm just mincing words, but stick with me for a moment. If I call you and you tell me, "I'm just not ready yet," or "Now's not a good time," and I say, "Not a problem. When would you like me to get back in touch?" Most sales people would accept a blow off such as "tomorrow" or "next week" or "next month" or "next quarter."

Instead of accepting that non-committal answer, press for a specific date and time. "Tomorrow? No problem. What time works for you?" Sure, they may be in a rush at that moment, but aren't we all? And is their time any more valuable than yours? Stand your ground and ask for a time. "2 PM tomorrow? Got it. I'll call you at 2 tomorrow. Have a good day."

Now, when I call her back at 2 PM tomorrow, I'm not "following up." We have an appointment. When the gate-keeper/receptionist/executive assistant asks, "May I ask what this call is regarding?" or "Is she expecting your call?", you can honestly reply with, "Yes. I'm calling for our 2 PM appointment."

See the difference?
Your demeanor will be different.

Whomever answers the phone will treat you differently. The prospect will be more respectful of your time. Everyone wins.

As an added bonus, if the prospect stands you up, you can leave a voicemail message that says "I was just calling in for our 2 PM appointment. Please let me know when you'd like to resume our conversation." You now have the moral high ground because they stood you up for an appointment they agreed to have.

Now do you understand why I say "Life's too short for follow-up calls"? ~✲~

Why are these prospecting phones always so dang big and heavy and hard to pick up?

www.TheSalesWhisperer.com

Reaching The Stars

36 years 29 days ago, a 1,588 pound (721.9 kg) blinking gizmo was perched precisely 157 feet (47.8 metres) atop enough Nitrogen Tetroxide, Aerozine, Liquid Oxygen and Liquid Hydrogen to drown Huell in "Breaking Bad."

Why? To go where no man has gone before.

Back then—August 20, 1977—regular gas was just 62¢ per gallon (remember "regular" gas?) so nobody cared much about miles per gallon.

But all of that fuel—24,900 gallons in just one stage of a Titan IIIe Centaur—was lit on fire to propel the blinking gizmo to where no man or woman has gone before.

The gizmo was the Voyager 2 satellite, which passed Pluto and departed our heliosphere—Elvis has left the building! So, the Voyager 2 satellite has traveled over 11,000,000,000 (that's eleven billion) miles, and it is still going 36 years later with no more than 16 minutes of fuel at any time. That's 441,767 miles per gallon. (And you thought the Chevy Volt got good mileage.)

"That's wonderful, Wes...I guess. But why are you telling me this? Have you been helping one of your 22 children with their science fair project or something?"

I tell you this to encourage you to continue developing your plans that may still be on the launchpad or just in the design phase. The beginning and the planning and the behind-the-scenes toiling are the hardest part of any new endeavor. (NASA's budget in 1977 was $11,668,000 in 2007 dollars so go easy on yourself if you're still bootstrapping your own launch.)

It takes a big effort for a focused amount of time to build momentum. What you do today and tonight and in the early morning hours tomorrow can carry you through the rest of your life. But you have to plot a course, set a goal, begin the work and stick with it through to launch because until you launch, you don't know how good or bad your idea is. Heck, even with all of that money, NASA had one out of seven launches fail.

If you need some help, let me know. Keep building, like Lori…
~*~

> "It was so great meeting you at Digi! Thank you so much for your session. I learned so much and can't wait to sit down and go over my notes and work on my business plans. I'm especially grateful that I had the chance to meet you before my upcoming speaking engagement. My plan for my talk has entirely changed and I know it's going to be so much more profitable now!
>
> You are such an inspiration! I'm very blessed to have heard your story and met you. Thanks again!"
>
> **Lori Bryant**
> **www.hairbylori.com**
>
> P.S. I converted 38 out of 88 on my very first talk. That's 43% of the room. I feel so encouraged and even more motivated about getting out there and speaking again.

You Cannot Climb a Smooth Mountain

When you're in your respective "valleys" that life throws at you more often than you think it should, it's good to keep in mind what it really takes to reach the pinnacle of success.

If you'd like to climb to 29,028 feet, you can do one of two things:

Go to the nearest airport and plunk down $199 (+ baggage fees and security fees and food fees and fee fees...what a bunch of feces, huh!) and in about 90 minutes you'll be at 29,028 feet...
- enjoying a book,
- a movie,
- a nap,
- the crossword puzzle,
- a little sip of your favorite beverage

...along with 154 other flip-flop-wearing, over-stimulated, under-focused, non-journey-enjoying travelers, who are either temporarily going where they want to go or temporarily escaping where they are tired of being.

OR...

- Go to the gym daily for 730 days;
- take mountaineering courses to learn about survival, routes, equipment, & diet;
- practice climbing on smaller mountains for 2-3 years and make sure your practice includes steep faces, high terrain, night climbing, ice & snow;
- plunk down $25,000 to $60,000 (for extra goats to keep you warm at night);
- prepare for sudden extremes, like winds stronger than Cat 2 hurricanes and temperatures cold enough to make Paris Hilton put on clothes;
- fast forward to actually arriving in country where you'll climb to 5 camps at subsequently higher levels as you...
- acclimate yourself,

- test your equipment and
- monitor the environmentals to increase your chances of success.

The day you decide to go you must leave before sunrise with ample gear, a good guide and a belly full of determination. (And you thought calling on some grumpy prospects was hard! HA! What time did you get up today?)

Your climb to the top requires—necessitates, demands—"base camps," ledges, plateaus to help you catch your breath, examine your situation, and build strength for the effort you must exert to reach the next level. If you move too quickly, your body will not acclimate and you will pass out or get sick and be forced to go down one or more levels or quit altogether. If you move too slowly, bad weather can strike and force you down or kill you or you'll run out of money and supplies, which will force you to quit.

See the similarities to reaching your business goals?

Trees do not grow to the sky, stocks do not go straight up, and businesses do not grow without plateaus and even setbacks.

If business is down today, is it because you did not adequately train and prepare? Did you move too fast, thinking the laws of business and finance and marketing did not apply to you? Did you move too slowly, maybe out of timidity or insecurity, or because you did not have a great sherpa to show you the way?

Are you "stuck" at a basecamp today? If you view your basecamp as a place for losers and the weak, you will soon find yourself weak and losing. Conversely, if you view them as places of rest and planning that empower you to prepare for the exciting opportunities ahead, you will not only enjoy the journey, you will most assuredly reach your summit.

Any fool that's collected aluminum cans for a few weeks can afford an $89 plane ticket to get a Coke and a smile and some honey roasted peanuts while perusing "Sky Mall" magazine.
Real adventurers take the "road less travelled," and see the jagged edges and plateaus as toeholds and places of rejuvenation. And they always have a sherpa to guide them.

How high do you want to go...and do you have a sherpa to assist you?

I'm happy to provide you with this written guide and to be your sherpa, if you'll allow me as Laura has… ~*~

Is Coffee Really For Closers?

"Put. That coffee. Down. Coffee's for closers only."

What an unfortunate line.

It was uttered with great effect—and impact—by Alec Baldwin who played a tough-nosed sales manager in the 1992 movie "Glengarry Glen Ross."

I say it's unfortunate because it continues to guide how new salespeople think they should act despite its near-30 years in the lexicon.

But that's not the worst of it.

This movie is based on a 1983 play by David Mamet that won the Pulitzer Prize in 1984.

So this quote, this adage, this concept is closer to 40 years old.

But that's not the worst of it.

The play is based on Mamet's experience working in a real estate office in the 1970s where he was the office manager responsible for handing out sales leads.

So this quote, this adage, this concept is closer to 50 years old…yet it continues to shape and mold the sales industry to this day.

But now, with the power of Artificial Intelligence, we know that the money is not made in the close. It's made in how you open, how you engage in dialogue, and how you help your prospects build their confidence.

We know that because of people like Chris Orlob over at Gong.io, who analyzed 25,537 B2B sales conversations with AI and discovered five critical points pertaining to opening, closing, and professional selling.

In a nutshell, coffee is for openers, for humans, for non-closers.

So enjoy the movie.

Enjoy your coffee.

.ₛₛ$$$$$$$$ $ $ $ $ $$$$$ₛₛ

Enjoy being a human in the profession of sales, which will help
you enjoy opening a lot more relationships…and overflowing bank
accounts. ~✶~

P.S. Do yourself a favor and listen to my interview with Chris
on The Sales Podcast at **TheSalesWhisperer.com/session233**.

*"Wes has become an integral part of our sales training. We met
in 2009 at the Infusionsoft conference and we have been
working together ever since.*

*"His approach is very straight forward and has really helped
me and my sales team to gain more appointments, more
commitments toward closing and of course more sales.*

*"I love when one of my sales people come in and says, 'I used
one of Wes' tools today and it really worked!' Thanks for all
the help Wes, looking forward to next month!"*

**Laura Wrasman
Owner, Wedding Guide Chicago – Chicago, IL**

The New ABCs of Selling

Alec Baldwin made another sales saying infamous in "Glengarry Glen Ross" when he flipped over his chalkboard to reveal two acronyms on sales, with the first being…

"A-B-C. A, always; B, be; C, closing. Always be closing! Always be closing!"

But as evidence-based research has shown us—thanks to people like Chris Orlob and his team at Gong.io—this is not how to make every sale. (Do yourself a favor and listen to my interview with Chris on The Sales Podcast. You can access the interview and my notes at **TheSalesWhisperer.com/session233**.)

This is why I say there is a new set of ABCs when it comes to professional selling today, and they include:

- **Always Be Concise:** your prospects have information. What they need is knowledge, wisdom, answers. Help them find their own truth as it pertains to their needs, timelines, abilities, and budget by giving answers they can understand and engaging them with questions they're too inexperienced to even ask.

- **Always Be Courteous**: does this even need explaining? (To be honest, this is for me more than it is for you. I can lose my cool when I'm dealing with those who are controlling, narcissistic, or who hide their inability to invest with me by being overly-analytical or critical. But I digress.)
- **Always Be Curious**: Curiosity may kill cats, but not knowing all the facts kills deals, which kills the careers of thousands of careless, overly-confident salespeople every year. In fact, "Assumption Malfunction" is #4 of **"The 7 Deadly Sins of Selling."** If you don't know something, ask. or update your resume.
- **Always Be Confident**: Regardless your industry, you are selling confidence. Your prospects are swamped with data. They need you to let them know they are making the right decision. So know your stuff. Know yourself. Know how to conduct yourself in every sales encounter. That takes practice. That's what you will learn in The Make Every Sale Community. Join today at **www.MakeEverySale.com**.
- **Always Be Connecting**: If you know the right people and the right people know you, you won't have to make cold calls or waste time and money on marketing campaigns that are too complex to be effective. Get out and get known.
- **Always Be Calm**: See **"Always Be Confident."**
- **Always Be Cautious**: A deal is not a deal until the order is placed and the check has cleared the bank. Being optimistic is fine, as long as you're cautiously optimistic. In the book "Extreme Ownership," retired Navy SEAL Jocko Willink (in the Victory MMA shirt to the right with me) describes how he would ambush his men in training on their way home from an exercise, which is when the average fighter would let his guard down, thinking their planned engagement was over and now it's time to head to the house. Your deal can die at any time—even after the order is placed—so stay cautious.

Master these ABCs of Selling and you'll then be ready for the new ABCDEs of Selling, which begin…now! ~✶~

The New ABCDEs of Selling

Is selling a "funnel" or a "pipeline" or a "throw-enough-crap-against-the-wall-something-is-bound-to-stick"?

What if it's none of the above? What if it's some of all of the above…plus a little something extra?

Old school sales trainers tell you that

- "Coffee is for closers" and
- "You should focus 80% of your sales effort on the close, because that's where the sale is made" and
- "The sale begins when you hear 'No!'" and
- "Just keep your pipeline full and good things will happen!"

How's all that wonderful, timeless advice working for you and your team?

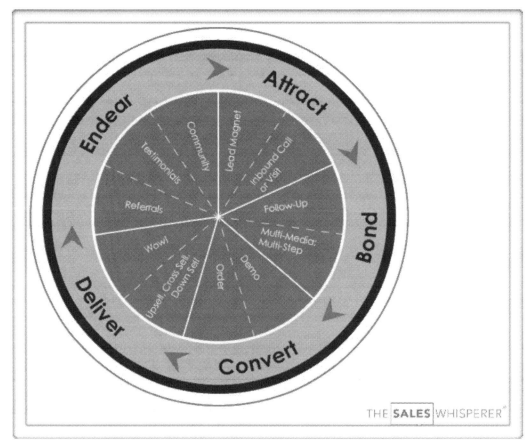

Rookie salespeople think that their job is done once the sale is made. (They also think they can do it all alone, which is why they're rookies.)

Professional salespeople, sales managers, business owners, and entrepreneurs understand that how you do anything is how you do everything (and that the hip bone is connected to the leg bone, …which will make sense in a minute.)

Professionals understand that we do judge books by their covers. They understand that people buy from those we know, like, and trust. They know that simply providing $100 of service in exchange for $100 is not memorable, exceptional, or anything other than just not illegal. Finally, professional salespeople understand that birds of a feather flock together and that it's much easier and more profitable to make a repeat sale to a happy customer—and their friends—than to make a new sale to a cold prospect.

With these understandings in mind, allow me to introduce you to The A.B.C.D.E. Sales & Marketing System™.

- **Attract:** visitors to your website, store, booth and offer them something so attractive they identify themselves so you can…
- **Bond:** ideally multi-media, multi-step, which requires the right CRM and marketing automation. (Might I recommend my free tool at **BestCRMQuiz.com?**) Once you've bonded it's easy to…
- **Convert:** them to paying **customers.** But now the real work begins. This is when you…
- **Deliver:** a "WOW" experience. **Delight** them so you then…
- **Endear:** yourself to them. When you have happy clients Tweeting about you and giving you 5-star reviews on Google, Yelp, and Facebook, their friends and people like them will notice, which begins the **Attract** stage again, but this time it's even easier.

Notice in the picture above that this is not a one-direction top-down funnel or a left-to-right pipeline. This is a cycle. A never-ending cycle that, when handled properly, leads to an acceleration of your sales, even at higher margins, because when you understand and master the fundamentals—and what is more fundamental than your ABCDEs?—sales really do become easy and predictable.

But—and there's always a "but!"—this is easier said than done. But I can promise you it's worth doing and will pay dividends for years, if not the rest of your selling career. ~✱~

One Step Forward, No Steps Back

Do you know what makes the **CLANK! CLANK! CLANK!** sound when you're going up the roller coaster lift hill? (Did you even know that first hill was called a lift hill? Me neither. Thank you **DuckDuckGo.** No, Google is not my default search engine because they spy on you. And I also interviewed the founder of DuckDuckGo, Gabriel Weinberg, on The Sales Podcast #197. We discussed the four steps to launch, why you need to own the customer acquisition plan, what Google really is, and the importance of testing even though most tests fail, among other things. You can listen in on our conversation and read my notes at **www.TheSalesWhisperer.com/session197**. Now back to our roller coaster and the CLANK!)

The thing that makes that sound is called an **anti-rollback dog.** According to Wikipedia it's "a rack (ratcheted track) alongside the chain to prevent the train from descending the lift hill." Related to the **anti-rollback dog** are the **chain dogs.** "**Chain dogs** underneath each train are engaged by the chain and the train is pulled up the lift." (Don't ask my why roller coaster builders love dogs, but I think that makes them pretty cool, as if they weren't cool enough already for building roller coasters. I mean, come on!)

As a rider of roller coasters you should be thrilled to know there are safety measures in place to ensure your car does not slide backwards and injure or kill you and your loved ones.

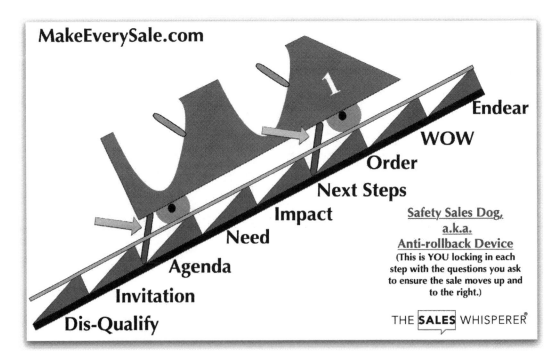

But how do you keep your sales opportunities from sliding backwards? What proven processes and safety measures have you implemented to ensure it's not two steps forward and one step back as you move your leads through The A.B.C.D.E. Sales & Marketing System™?

What's that? You just learned about The A.B.C.D.E. Sales & Marketing System™ two pages ago and haven't implemented it, yet? Well what are you waiting for?

Okay, okay. You can finish this section first, but then I really need you to get to work on this. It's for your own good. I'll wait for you to finish. If you have questions or want to give me an update on how it's going, head on over to my free group at **TheImplementors.com.** It's for those of us who implement, need a mentor, and are willing to mentor other motivated sales professionals.

Now let's get back to the Sales Dog.

For example, here's a question posted in **TheImplementors.com** group just yesterday:

> *"Hey Wes....when you have someone say 'I just need to talk to my spouse' and want to follow up with them what objections do I need to overcome?'"*

Old school sales trainers tell you to focus 80% of your time and energy on overcoming objections, because they think that is where the sale is made. I think that's how exhaustion and animosity in made! If you are getting an objection like this, it's too late. Like buying stocks or businesses or property, you make your money going in, thus my motto **"Close First. Then Present."**

If you've been selling for more than a minute you know what objections you're going to get so it is foolish and amateurish (are those redundant) to not prepare for—and address—these objections before they arise because if you can eliminate all objections ahead of time, the sale can't slide backwards, thus you are the ultimate **Sales Dog!**

Going back to Sarah's question in **TheImplementors.com**, here's how I responded:
That sucks. You have to prevent it from coming up in the first place. Here's how the conversation would go:

> *"So Sarah, when it comes to making decisions like this, who on your team/in your family do you consult/bounce ideas off of for their insight and opinion?"*

"Well Wes, I always bring in my spouse/CFO/IT director/attorney/CPA."

"Fantastic, what would it take to have them at the meeting, you know, so we can save time and avoid the telephone game. You know how that goes, right? You get excited and want to move forward but as you try to explain it to that key person things get lost in translation. I mean, it happens. I've been doing this 22 years and you're trying to convey a major concept after maybe 22 minutes. Do you have access to their calendar? I'll wait."

The real close here is on getting the influencer to attend the meeting. When I sold life insurance I NEVER met with one spouse. They NEVER "make all the decisions." So I spent time on the phone probing for answers to the main issues that could derail the sale such as them having the time to meet, who the real decision-makers are, their decision-making process, competitors, budget, pain, and desire to make a change.

As I discover, address, and eliminate each of the deal-killers I am slowly moving up the lift (sales) hill and engaging my Sales Dog after each one.
- You sound like a reasonable/rational human being that will be easy to work with? **CLANK!**
- Your spouse/partner will be present? **CLANK!**
- Your insurance rates are going up so you need to make a change this month/quarter? **CLANK!**
- Your spouse/partner agrees that you need to make a change? **CLANK!**
- We can meet at your office while the kids are at school and your spouse can meet us there for an hour? **CLANK!**
- You've told me how much you're spending now and/or how much your rates are increasing? **CLANK!**
- You've shared with me your top 2-3 non-negotiable criteria for making a decision and I meet all of them? **CLANK!**
- You've told me who the other competitors are and I know I can beat them? **CLANK!**

You see how this works? Rookie salespeople hear someone say "Yes, I'll meet with you" and run out to buy a new Tesla! A deal's not done until the deal is done, the check has cleared, the customer has received the product/service, they've stated they are thrilled with your assistance, they are giving you a glowing testimonial along with ideal referrals, and they are placing repeat orders. **CLANK! CLANK! CLANK! CLANK!**
Stop chasing waterfalls and butterflies.

Have the guts and the wisdom to ask a few more tough questions before at the beginning of the relationship so you know if there is even a relationship to be had.

That's how professional salespeople conduct business, and that's what'll make you a true Sales Dog. CLANK! CLANK! WOOF! WOOF! Now go close first, then present. ~*~

Hey, sidebar:

This has nothing to do with this chapter. I have so much content spilling out of my computer I could write more than a few 1,000 books, but who the heck would read a single book that long, let alone several?

So I figured I'd sprinkle in some additional lessons where I have room, so here's the first of **The 7 Deadly Sins of Selling** and it applies to the woman pictured here.

Her name is Annie Oakley and she was an amazing trick shot artist who got her start around 1885.

As you can see, she could shoot over her shoulder with a mirror, which was quite entertaining. She could also **shoot from the hip** without looking.

But she practiced that technique until she couldn't miss.

How many of your sales calls, emails, voicemails, trade shows, proposals, networking events, and meetings are done in the spur of the moment, with no forethought, just shooting from the hip?

How much is that costing you? Want to beat all seven of these deadly sales sins for free? Get my on-demand video series while it's still offered for no charge at **bit.ly/7DeadlyFree**.

Now go sell something.

Handling the Biggest Stall of the Fall!

Whether you're a top-performing salesperson shooting for #1, or you're behind on your numbers and you're fighting for your life, salespeople dread making calls during the holidays. Your clients and prospects, who are not good at making decisions in the first place, use the holidays as a convenient excuse to keep their heads buried in places that are quite dark and not very spacious.

"Call you after the New Year?" AHHHHHHH!

What's really going to change after we spend 38 days:

- traveling, eating, and watching football?
- pretending to be excited to see 23 people we wish could only see once a DECADE?
- looking for AA batteries?
- hiding from kids armed with too many toys powered by those AA batteries?
- making another New Year's resolution we know we'll break before the Orange Bowl?

"Give me a call after the holidays" is not an objection. It's far more insipid. It's a put-off. A stall. A think-it-over.

Stalls are DEATH to salespeople. Time kills deals! Stalls make you dance. Put-offs make you poke and prod to uncover the truth because you cannot proceed until the truth is uncovered.

While it's best to PREVENT the stall from ever rearing its ugly head, here are a handful of tips, witty responses and clever lines that may actually have you looking forward to the previously-dreaded, "Call me after the New Year."

1. **Soften the beach head, i.e. send cards and/or gifts and/or invitations to holiday parties…and do it early!** Over the last several years I've started sending Thanksgiving cards to beat the rush and the crush of holiday season. It sets me apart. It puts me out ahead of my competitors. It captures the attention of my clients and prospects. Just like an artillery barrage softens the beach so the Marines can land safely, a gift and/or invitation to a holiday party/meal makes the the recipient more receptive to taking my call or seeing me when I stop by. Send a real gift like candy or a fruit/cheese/meat basket or a funny gift like a fruitcake and a note like "The gift that keeps on giving….just like owning my **Infusionsoft book.** When can we schedule a time to answer your questions and help you invest your end-of-year funds wisely?"

2. **Drop the cat in the punch bowl.** In my training I help people eliminate "Think It Overs" by taking that away from them right up front with a solid **sales agenda.** In that scenario you tell the prospect "If you're tempted to say you want to think it over is it ok if I take that as you not wanting to hurt my feelings and we can just put you down as a 'no'?" Do the same thing here. Ask them "are you just trying to be nice and not hurt my feelings or do you really have an interest in our offerings?" If you get a bunch of "no's" during this time you'll know how hard you'll have to work come Jan 1 to make your numbers…or you'll have time to start looking for a new job over the Christmas break!

3. **Life's too short for follow-up calls.** If the answer to #2 is to your liking, press for a firm date and time to speak or meet. One of my tag lines for years has been "Life's too short for follow-up calls." If you simply say "Ok, I'll call you after the 1st," that prospect has forgotten you before they hang up. Follow-ups are deadly because they are one-sided "appointments" that only you set, which means they will wear you out. That's why the next step must be scheduled and mutually agreed to or you'll never reach them. Now when you call or stop by you are doing so because you have an appointment, which is significantly different from a

lowly little follow-up call.

4. **Use dynamite…er…humor.** Humor is like dynamite: a little goes a long way. If you've made it this far and are still engaged in verbal jarring and positioning, the prospect may be a little tense/short-tempered. Diffuse the situation with a smidgen of humor. A little personality goes a long way toward establishing trust and getting past put-offs and stalls.

> **"How's August 18th next year?** I've had so many clients and prospects hit me with the 'after the holiday objections' that I'm completely booked until mid-August! Can you believe that? You can beat the rush by meeting now and as luck would have it, I have a few openings between now and December 31st. Whadaya say?"
> **Lottery winner.** "You're the 37th person to tell me that today, which means you get to have lunch with me and you get to name your price—within reason of course. What are you in the mood for?"

5. **Stand your ground.** "Mr. Prospect, for us both to have a happy holiday an order needs to be placed here. I need the sale and you need this decision off of your plate and your company needs the benefits of what we offer. Why delay any longer?"

6. **Go "Columbo."** "Excellent idea. Why spoil the egg nog with business now, right? Let me ask you something while I'm here: What will be different after New Year's Day? Is it a budget thing or is there something looming on the horizon that could make you unable to order? (Your prospect will say, "Oh no. Not at all.") "Whew! What a relief! You know how busy we get this time of year with last-minute orders. Why don't we jump the line and get your order in the queue so you can get this off your plate, schedule the exact delivery, which we can guarantee if you order now, and even split up your payments or not invoice you until the last day or first day of the year, whichever meets your accounting needs?"

7. **Mix and match.** I can't tell you how many times we got creative at the end of the year when I was selling in the technology space. We split orders into hardware and software and even installation and warranties. We took huge orders at the end of the year in return for a larger discount with delivery scheduled throughout the first quarter or even all of the next year. Even now I'll offer split payments on the Infusionsoft setup and even have clients get started with a lower package so they can get their contacts imported and

some Campaigns built and running, which will allow them to cancel other subscriptions they may be paying for such as ConstantContact or HubSpot or 1ShoppingCart, then take those savings and apply them to a larger Infusionsoft application. There's more than one way to skin a cat, especially at the end of the year.

8. **Sell on price…**

   By discounting: If you need the sale, open yourself up to aggressive discounts. It's not ideal but neither is being broke. "We are having a 30% off December sale. Our biggest of the year!"

   By raising your prices: Most companies raise their prices after the first of the year so inform your prospects that a list price purchase now will save them the 3-5-7-10% price increase coming right around the corner.

Pressure exposes weakness. In sales, there's no pressure like the end of year trifecta:

- End of Month.
- End of Quarter.
- End of Year.

Your pay, your bonuses, your prestige, company trips and awards, maybe even raises, promotions and/or your job may be at stake based on how you handle this important time of the year. But just like your physical health, your selling health can't be "fixed" in a short, concentrated burst of activity. If an out-of-shape person jumps into the Iron Man contest, not only will they not finish the race, they'll probably get injured, and might actually die.

The same is true for selling.

If you are not in touch with your clients and prospects on a regular basis you do not have a strong, healthy relationship with them because healthy relationships are built on trust, which is built on communication.

If you are getting these stalls it means your clients are "seeing someone else" because you are not providing the frequency and the quality of communication they expect, want and deserve. (That's why I started using Infusionsoft back in 2008 then moved both my Wordpress website, inbound marketing, CRM, and marketing automation to HubSpot in 2014 to coordinate my marketing and sales.)

Life's too short for follow-up calls and it's too short to sweat the sale at all, let alone during what should be your downtime, your family time, your time to give thanks, your time to eat turkey, drink eggnog, celebrate a special birthday from 2000 years ago, and ring in the New Year.

Get ahead of the curve by planning, by being consistent and even aggressive in your marketing 52 weeks a year so you can actually take the end of the year off to enjoy your family (that's why you're doing all you do, right?), recharge your batteries and even do some goal-setting and planning for the New Year.

Merry Christmas. ~✹~
(Inspired by Jeffrey Gitomer.)

Hey, sidebar:

Remember that story about Annie Oakley a few pages back? Start planning your year today. Create your sales and marketing campaign now because you know there will always be a President's Day and a Valentine's Day and a St. Patrick's Day, etc.

So why not think a few moves ahead of your competition to put yourself in position to beat them before they even get to the office?
Visit **www.HolidayInsights.com** for a list of all the fun, crazy, and interesting holidays for every day, week, and month of every year to give you some inspiration for your next promotion.

For example, we all know that Halloween and Oktoberfest are in October. How predictable and pedantic. Why not run a special for **"World Smile Day"** on the first Friday of the month or **"Boss's Day"** on the 16th or **"Make a Difference Day"** on the 4th Saturday?

Play chess while your competition is playing checkers.

Victory over the Vortex.

The whirlwind and the mission.
The vortex and the goal.
The ringing phone and the bigger picture.
Focusing on the former leads to feeling overwhelmed.
Being overwhelmed leads to feeling inadequate.
Feeling inadequate leads to giving up the dream.

"Overwhelmed and inadequate" is how a manager described his feelings after attending yet another rah-rah training program delivered by well-meaning readers-of-books who demonstrated their prowess at book-reading during the previous 48 hours and concluded their book-reading "training" by giving attendees even more books and binders to read for "continued self-improvement."

You and I both know those books, binders, CDs, DVDs, and notes end up becoming collectors of dust and guilt because they will never be touched by human hands until they are gently placed in the trash bin many moons from now...

...which leads to feeling more overwhelmed and inadequate.
All of my clients realize several things about business:

• It's easy to start a business.

- It's hard to run a business.
- It's almost impossible to succeed at business.
- Until you succeed, you're the loneliest person on Earth.
- Even after you succeed, only fellow-business owners truly understand you.

You can only succeed when you develop systems and processes and surround yourself with excellence because…

- There is a lot to do.
- You cannot do it all.
- Others can do the busywork for you if you train and allow them.
- Your clients are happy with what your staff can do as long as they know it's done under your watchful eye.
- Your eye remains keen and sharp and fresh and productive when it is not tired and blurred with the tears of exhaustion and frustration that always come when you try to do it all yourself.

"Doing it all" was bad enough before the Internet and technology "made our lives simpler and paperless." (Your life is simpler and paperless now, right?)

Now we must wrestle and wrangle with a slew of tools and sites and acronyms that we cannot define, let alone leverage—SaaS, CRM, SMS, MMS, PPC, SEM, SEO, CSS, HTML, PHP, JV, ADD, ADHD, OCD, ED, ROFLMAO, RUOK, BFF, WTH, SMH.

So we wrangle and grapple and run and hide from this vortex because we do not want to appear ignorant and we do not / cannot spend a ton of money on some pointy-headed, fast-talking "guru" to confuse us some more.

What salespeople, business owners and entrepreneurs need is a reliable, effective, measurable, repeatable, affordable way to deliver a powerful message in a powerful manner. We need access to capable technicians and advisors to assist with the development and the dissemination of that message. And we need a place where we can mingle and brainstorm and "brain-still" with our peers, behind closed doors, away from the watchful, prying eyes of "the marketplace" to rejuvenate our spirits and put a spring back in our steps.

It's normal to be consumed by the vortex at times. It's normal to wonder if the goal is really worth the effort. It's normal to feel guilty about investing more money in training or consulting or workshops or conferences or coaches. It's normal for your company to not want to pay for it. It's normal to be mad about that. It's ABNORMAL to do it anyway and to feel good about yourself. To have faith and confidence that the only sure investment is an investment in yourself.

So keep kissing guru-frogs until you find a good one and until you become a guru in your own right. Trust me, you are better than you give yourself credit for. You have more knowledge and insight and skills and intuition than you realize. Give yourself permission to rest and give yourself permission to excel.

You are not alone. People like you are why I developed an institute of higher business, sales and marketing learning that convenes regularly in the wine country of Southern California. The good weather, great wine, exceptional learning and lifelong friendships make the programs worth the walk, drive, flight, boating or hot-air ballooning it will take for you to get here.

Regardless of where you find your reprieves and your inspiration, remember to "sell different." ~*~

Hey, sidebar:

In a previous life I was in the financial industry. It was a short-lived career so I won't bore you with the details, but one little nugget—or patty—has remained with me since 1997.

One of the senior advisors there asked me *"Wes, do you know why most advisors aren't rich? They don't believe their own bullshit."* I have followed that advice when considering investments ever since.

In 2006 I was given that advice by my sales mentor who told me *"Wes, be a product of your product."* I followed his advice and my sales grew.

In 2008, when I bought Infusionsoft for myself and starting helping others with it, I became a product of the product, and my business grew.

Are you selling Fords but driving a Chevy? Are you selling PCs but use a Mac? Do you yell "Roll Tide Roll!" but try to eat with utensils? (Oooh, that might be a low blow. I might consider putting myself into timeout for that one…maybe.)

Freedom is when what you believe, say, and do are all the same. So get your shit together and watch your business boom.

Will This Be the Year You Tame Your "Tiger?"

Conventional wisdom marks 2:25 AM, Nov 27, 2009 as the moment Tiger Woods' "life" came to an end. But how often is conventional wisdom correct? I propose that history will show that 11/27/09 is the morning Tiger finally began living.

"Aurgh?" I hear you say. (There are secret microphones in the book. Remember my buddy who's a general in the Air Force? Yeah. He has lots of cool technology he lets me play with. But don't tell anybody, okay?) *"How in the world can the moment the biggest athlete in the cosmos was exposed to be a fatally flawed individual (like the rest of us) be a good thing?"* (I told you I can hear you.09)

Great questions. (Even the Aurgh.)

Previously I wrote about "Victory Over The Vortex." While Tiger faced a public, outer vortex, it was just that—public and on the outside. (Something about sticks and stones comes to mind.) It is nothing compared to the inner, private, conflicted and self-inflicted vortex that had dominated and been parasitically destroying his life for many years before that fateful night.

Meanwhile, the world watched his saga unfold by the minute in much the same way we macabrely slow down to look at a wreck on the side of the road.

We're curious.
We don't want to see anything bad.
We do want to see something bad.
We're relieved it's not us.
We give thanks it's not us.
We criticize those in the wreck saying,
"What were they thinking?"
"How can they be so stupid?"
"How can they be so careless?"
"What in the heck..." BAMM!!

And we slam into the car in front of us, thereby creating the next spectacle to further distract and slow down traffic. How and why did this happen?

Because we took our eye off the goal, shifted our focus and filled our thoughts with self-righteous indignation at how silly and foolish and knuckleheaded everyone else is,

forgetting for that brief moment that "There, but for the grace of God, go I."
We all have our own vortices, which we must isolate and circumnavigate to avoid becoming discombobulated until we are able to at least minimize, if not vaporize, these spinning traps. But first we must acknowledge them.

Four members of my family have been through Alcoholics Anonymous. All of them had to stand up, in public, and say, "Hello, my name is ____, and I'm an alcoholic."

POW!

It is stated that 50% of the healing comes right then. Right there. By simply uttering nine words. Nine words that take between three seconds and 40 years to say, makes the utterer halfway healed.

ARE YOU halfway over your biggest challenges?

I hear you saying, "I'm so glad this year / this quarter / this month / this week is over," to which I ask, "Really? Why?"

What are you committing to RIGHT NOW;
what plan of action are you putting into place RIGHT NOW;
what team of experts are you surrounding yourself with RIGHT NOW;
what obstacles are you removing RIGHT NOW;
what stupid television shows are you turning off RIGHT NOW so you can focus on productive work;
what stupid gossip are you closing your ears to RIGHT NOW;
what unhealthy foods are you putting down RIGHT NOW;
and what negative, counter-productive and self-defeating thoughts are you clearing out of your head RIGHT NOW to make sure next year is not only better than this year, but it is actually the best year of your entire life?

What are your vortices?
How long have you been shouldering them?
How big of a burden have they become?
When will you acknowledge them?
When will you get help addressing them?
When will you get help conquering them?
When will you cease to be satisfied with the chaos and unsatisfying results in the areas of your business and your life that matter most to you and get P.O.'d enough to finally take action?

We all have *vorticification* in our lives. Scientists even give it a word: entropy. It's the natural tendency for the universe to collapse into homogeneity.
It's the natural tendency of winners to conquer the *collapsification*.
Tiger conquered the tendency to collapse in golf tournaments. And despite his outward chaos and hoopla, on February 19, 2010, when Tiger Woods admitted his problems to the world, he became 50% healed of his internal demons.

When will you face the *chaosification* of your life?
When will you stop attempting to assuage your wounds by staring at the collapses of everyone else?

Your competition is either sucking their thumbs in anticipation of the end or they are hoping for some miraculous rescue (which ain't gonna happen) or they are aggressively, decisively and proactively moving forward to expand their marketshare and put the thumb suckers out of their misery.

Take decisive action like Nathan. You'll be glad you did. ~✭~

Would You Like Some Fries With That?

What a simple question.
What a powerful question.
What a profitable question.
(Shhhh. It's also a script. But more on that later.)

The right idea…the right question..the right program…the right offer at the right moment can double your sales quicker than a knife fight in a phone booth. (Or faster than green grass through a goose.)

Alka Seltzer DOUBLED sales when, on the advice of Herta Herzog, a motivational researcher and marketing consultant, they changed their TV ads from showing one tablet being dropped into a glass water to two. ("Plop. Plop. Fizz. Fizz. Oh what a…") Southwest Airlines added $100 million in annual revenues by offering 15 passengers each flight to buy their new Business Select class, to which I've contributed more than a few dollars.)

But the average and ordinary are comfortable. They are not looking for ways to double sales.

"Double sales? DOUBLE SALES!? Haven't you seen the news you dang sales whisperer consulting dude? We're in a RECESSION!! (Or there will be one soon!) We're in a trade war with China. (Or we will be in one soon!) We're just focused on HANGIN' ON! HANGIN' ON, ya heard me? Double sales. What are you smokin'? Come back next year."

I know it was a tough adjustment after the 2008 collapse and I correctly predicted we would have a tough time for longer than most of the pundits wanted to admit. But I also think our economy—both domestically and internationally—and the buying habits of the world, have changed forever.
"Those who expect moments of change to be comfortable and free of conflict have not learned their history." ~Joan Wallach Scott

If you are willing to get up a little earlier, work a little smarter, seek the council of those with expertise beyond that of your own, craft your unique selling proposition, train your staff better, raise your expectations of everyone around you, challenge the status quo, take a fresh look at everything you do, and question every belief about sales and marketing you currently hold —this can be the best year of your professional life.
But if you approach business and life with an attitude of fear…

..₅$$$$$$$$$$$$$$$$$$₅₅.

If you are settling into your "prevent defense"…

If your fear of loss outweighs your desire to take bold action, well...

"Fear of loss, a path to the dark side is." ~Yoda

To continue on your journey to greatness, simply finish reading this book then review the **Resources** section at the back of the book and spend some quality, focused time browsing the additional materials I provide for free such as The Sales Podcast and The CRM Sushi Podcast, the Sales Agenda, the SlideShare presentations, The Weekly Whisper, and more. Maybe invest in "The 7 Deadly Sins of Selling" or "Making Good Money In Bad Times" CDs I sell for a few bucks or decide to jump head first into a training or coaching program you think you can't afford and watch what happens.

Money loves speed. Success favors the bold.

Here's wishing you the gift of focused, bold, decisive action. ~✶~

Hey, sidebar:

Do you know how long you have to be bold on a sales call or in a negotiation? Somewhere between three to seven seconds. That's how long it takes to ask the question that really matters then shut up and take notes.

Prospect: "Thanks but we're satisfied with our current vendor."

> **Average Salesperson:** "Oh…okay. Bye."

> **Professional Salesperson:** "Mr. Prospect, when you first chose your current supplier was the goal to be just satisfied or overjoyed?"

Prospect: "Thanks but we don't have the budget right now."

> **Average Salesperson:** "Oh…okay. Bye."

> **Professional Salesperson:** "Ms. Prospect, I know you don't have the budget. That's exactly why I called. What are you

implementing this quarter to ensure this doesn't happen next quarter?"

Prospect: "Can you send me some information?"

Average Salesperson: "Oh sure. Right away. Thank you so much. You're going to love what I send." (I'll be sure to follow-up incessantly and show you as a qualified opportunity on my pipeline for at least two quarters before I realize you're blowing me off and I'm a terrible salesperson.)

Professional Salesperson: "Joe, do you really want some information or are you just trying to be polite and not say 'no' because you think I'm going to try to turn it around and go for the hard close?"

Be present. Ask the questions that need to be asked. Listen for the answer. That's what I teach live, in-person every week in The Make Every Sale Community. Come join us at **www.MakeEverySale.com**.

> "The gatekeeper, chuckled and said 'Well at least you're honest.'
> "And after I gave her the 27 second spiel, she gave me the cell phone number of the manager."
>
> ~Nathan Brown

Do You Have Friends In Low Places?
(Are they helping you build your business?)

In July 1990 I had just finished my Sophomore year at the Air Force Academy. Being a smooth-talker, I lined up a sweet six-week gig as a training instructor in San Antonio, TX just 90 minutes from my adopted hometown of Houston, which essentially tripled my time at home that summer.

At the same time, Garth Brooks came out with his Sophomore album—he was following my college career—"No Fences," which included his hit single, "Friends in Low Places." That album in general, and this song, in particular, made Garth Brooks a superstar and it made me a dancing star at the only decent watering hole in Colorado Springs, Cowboys on North Tejon.

(Sidebar: Before you go poo-pooing country dancing, it's how I met my wife. So if your love life is lacking, you may want to look into taking some lessons. I'm just saying.)

Everyone—EVERYONE—knew Garth Brooks. He had crossed the line from country to pop and he was *hot*. "Friends in Low Places" was the anthem of the early 90's. His song resonated because we were coming out of the "Yuppie" decade of the 80's with all of its pomp and circumstance and BMW's and people thought it was now cool to be down-to-earth.

And it was.

However, when you listen to the words of this big hit, you may find it's a little sad. Garth is singing about being down and out. He's blue and sad. He's left out and forgotten and he's turning to whiskey and beer and friends in low places to forget how miserable he is. (Misery loves company, right?)

Let me ask you something: How many good ideas did you get from miserable friends in low places?

How abundant are low places filled with miserable people?

How often are you allowing yourself to be lured into the stinkin'-thinkin' oasis filled with friends in low places because it's easy?

Because your head hurts from thinking too much?
Because your heart hurts from struggling so much?
Because your forehead hurts from banging it against so many dead ends you've had to cross off on your journey to significance?

And all you want is an escape.

A temporary reprieve from the grind of your sales and entrepreneurial life. A cold drink, some hot wings and a good game on the "Tele" to numb the senses for a moment or three.

Let me ask you another question: How's that working out for ya?

While we all need to decompress from time to time, it should not become a habit, especially now. Now is the time to strike because your competition is weakened. Your prospects are open to new vendors and suppliers that can provide more value. They will respond to new offers, creative sales people and persistent business owners. They're tired of friends—and vendors—in low places.

You have competitors closing shop because the marketplace has shrunk and will continue to shrink for the average and ordinary. (And I hate to rain on your parade, but when the shrinking stops you will notice that consumers have been changed FOREVER by this first, truly hard time our nation has faced in over a generation. Please don't shoot the messenger, okay?)

So what are you doing right now, every week, every day, every hour to make sure you are positioned to take a larger percentage of business that your competition is either too weak, too dumb, too slow and/or too stuck in their ways to retain? What friends in low places do you need to leave behind?

What books are you reading? (Thanks for reading this one and getting this far. Keep going. You're on a roll and it gets better.) What conferences do you attend? What groups are you joining to keep you motivated, invigorated and your bank account populated?

None of us can succeed alone. John Wayne was a fictional character and he died in at least seven of his movies. But you're living and your goal is to live before you die, to achieve your goals, to reach your dreams.

Consider us at The Sales Whisperer® your friends in high places.

Here's to you living your dreams. ~✻~

Hey, sidebar:

Have you ever been to an MMA fight?

Have you ever been to an MMA fight out in the country?

Have you ever been to an MMA fight out in the country, in a converted garage, on a Sunday night, and parked in the dirt, and walked in the dark, past smelly port-o-johns and non-smelly food trucks to watch a friend step into the ring?

Have you ever been surrounded by people that don't look like you, dress like you, or even sound like you out in a field, at night, an hour from home, and most of them can fight?

Maybe you haven't lived until you have.

Look for the story later in this book with the title **"It's good to be punched in the face."**

You'll be glad you did.

And it might convince you to go make new friends.

The 10 Keys To Sales Success

We all love lists. Here are the 10 key components for sales success:

1. **Time Management**—Ask yourself: "Is what I'm doing right now the most productive and profitable thing I can be doing?" What this shows is that you cannot manage time but you can manage yourself. To see how you spend your time, track your daily actions in 15-minute increments for a month. You'll be shocked at how much time you waste and how much more efficient and effective you become.
(This is part of Lesson 1 in The Make Every Sale program. You can kick the tires for an entire month for next to nothing. Get started at **MakeEverySale.com** before you run out of time.)

2. **Raise Your Expectations**—Of everyone. Your employees, customers, your vendors, partners, your kids. Everyone. Do not demand more, but expect more and let them know you expect more.

3. **Think Big, Act Small**—Big goals are great but you have to take that first step towards that big goal.

4. **Take Massive Action**—There is no guarantee what will work, so you better be doing them all.

5. **Commit to Constant Improvement**—Just growing 1% today means you'll be 36% better at the end of the month. (Compounded growth is the 8th wonder of the world.)

6. **Deliver a Powerful Message In a Powerful Manner**—"The risk of insult is the price of clarity,"—Roy Williams. If you were arrested for being in sales and marketing, would there be enough evidence to convict you? Also, if you don't insult someone by noon, you're not marketing well enough.

7. **Disqualify Your Prospects**—Only 1-3% of the population at this exact moment in time is looking for what you are offering, know that they need it, and have the resources and desire to buy it from you today. So stop "qualifying" people when you prospect. You are looking for the guy looking for you. This subtle shift in mindset will help you live to sell day after day.

8. **Fix Your Follow-Up Failure**—Because 97-99% of people you meet today won't be able to buy from you today means you need to stay in touch because research has shown that 60-87% of

people that are shopping today will buy that product or service in 18-24 months. So you need a follow-up process, preferably one that's automated. Having processes and systems turned Ford into a household name. It will help you succeed as well. (I use www.BuyCRMNow.com to automate my sales and marketing and to fix my follow up failure.)

9. **Once The Sale Is Made, Shut Up**—Know when people are ready to buy and let them take possession of what you're offering. Just because you have an 87-slide presentation doesn't mean you have to give it all.

10. **Over-Deliver To Create Raving Fans**—Average and ordinary will not help you create a lasting business. To be "Facebookable" and Pinterest—worthy, choreograph your entire sales process from "Hello" to "Thank you for your order. How else may we be of service?" Then read their minds and provide that better, extra service without them asking.

Rest assured you will not be able to rest until you have systems in place that enable you to communicate with prospects and tire-kickers automatically and consistently tied to processes your team of professionals follows that ensure they engage with hot prospects and clients in a way that creates a "wow" experience and "delights to the upside."

But technology only enhances what you do, i.e. "Garbage in, garbage out." You must perfect your processes on paper before you turn to gizmos and geeks to load it into a CRM or email or social media marketing platform. In 1994, I started learning how to do this for my own success. It took me until 2006 to begin laying the foundation to help others shorten their learning curves.

Since the shortest distance between two points is a straight line, make a bee line over to TheSalesWhisperer.com to see how we can help you.

You deserve the best. I'll help you get there. But you have to not only decide to start, but actually start. ~*~

P.S. Every year since January 2015 I've braved the chilly waters of Tampa Bay to cross the 5 km to raise money for the Navy SEAL Foundation.

The money we raise goes to the families of our SEALs who are wounded or killed in the line of duty.

As we know, only the dead have seen the end of war. The families of the fallen must carry on and this event and this foundation lets them know they are not alone.

You can donate to my 3.1 mile / 5 km swim at **HelpWesSwim.org**.

You can learn about the swim at **www.tampabayfrogman.com**. Sponsors and volunteers are always welcomed.

You can learn about the well-run Navy SEAL Foundation at **www.navysealfoundation.org**. They are one of only 49 charities nationwide with a 100 score on fiscal management so you know your money is going to the families.

Pigs and Sharks

Sharks

In 1988, Harvey Mackay wrote the bestseller "Swim with Sharks Without Being Eaten Alive: Outsell, Outmanage, Outmotivate, and Outnegotiate Your Competition."

It was—and is—a good book on how to grow your business during a growing economy, a booming stock market, with clearly-understood competitors and no Internet.

Pigs

Around 2006, I read an even more powerful statement, "The pigs inside your business will destroy you far sooner than the sharks outside ever will."

ss$$$$$$$$$$$$$$$$$$$$s

The lazy, slothful, unappreciative employees that feel entitled to have a job and are left unattended, unsupervised, free to roam and do as they please inside your company do more harm than any competitor ever will.

Having seen this type of slothfulness more times than I can count in both Fortune 50 companies to the local insurance agency, I agree.

To address this you must **hire slow and fire fast**, which means you need systems and processes for recruiting, screening, interviewing, on-boarding, training, motivating and retaining your staff from the front office receptionist, to partners, to members of your board of directors.

In my No More Sales Duds program, www.NoMoreSalesDuds.com, I address how to do this in detail. It starts with adopting the mentality that you are always recruiting. Put a Careers tab on your website, put it on the back of your business card, offer bonuses to your staff when they refer good people that stick around at least 90 days.

In the job description section, avoid putting a job description. (AURGH?!) Put a Superstar Description. Describe the person you are looking for. Their attributes, motivations and key personality traits. Inform them you will be tough but supportive. Rigorous but fair. Focused but human.

It's like teaching an elementary school class. You can always ease up on the students and give them some leeway once you see them living up to the standards you have set for the class up front. But you can't show up with rainbows and unicorns and Capri Suns® and try to take it all away when they can't sit still and do their work because they're amped up on sugar.

When you are hiring anyone, especially salespeople, set the tone up front. Let them know the expectations you have of them and, as I've stated earlier, raise your level of expectations for everyone. Additionally, put the prospective sales person through a little test when they apply for the position. Be hard to reach. Tell them you're not sure they are what you're looking for. See how they respond. Do they cower and back down or do they buck up? If they buck up, which is what you want, how do they do it? You want sales people with backbones, but you want them with some couth and manners as well. Give them what they'll get in the real world of selling and see if they really are as good as their resume says.

When you hire them, support them with great sales training, which is NOT product training. Knowing the speeds and feeds of your latest gizmo is NOT sales training. Explaining to them the benefits of your new features, how your clients will use them to their benefit and how it impacts every person in your prospect's organization IS sales training. Providing them with scripts for prospecting calls IS sales training. Helping them set realistic short and long term goals IS sales training. Providing them with daily activity expectations and the tools and skills to execute them IS sales training.

This is how you keep both the pigs and the sharks at bay. (Do pigs swim in the bay?) There will always be competition and you want some. They'll keep you on your toes. So always take note of what the sharks at your competitors are up to, but spend more time focusing on where your staff is focusing.

That is, if you're in business to maximize your income. ~✻~

Hey, sidebar:

One day a little pig walked into a bar. He asked the bartender for a beer, and after drinking it he asked where the restroom was. The bartender told him and off walked the pig.

A second little pig walked in and also asked for a beer and directions to the restroom after drinking it. Once again the bartender gave directions and off walked the pig.

A third little pig walked into the bar and asked for a beer, which he also drank but then he just asked for the check. The bartender asked him, "Don't you want to know where the restroom is like your friends did?"

The pig replied, "No, I'm the little pig that went wee wee wee all the way home."

If you want to sell, then stories you must tell.

Besides, you can never have too many clean jokes in your arsenal.

As you can see I'm not hogging all the best ones, so I'm sure you're not boar-ed!

Okay, okay. No more ham-fisted pig jokes. I'm done with the puns.

New Economies Are Old

The "new normal" or the "new economy."

These phrases are kicked around every time there is a big enough shift in the economy to make the news, but the economy is always shifting. "Welcome to civilization and the human race." It's in our DNA to work, grow and progress.

Sure, the times, they are a-changin', and we will continue to see:

- Increased competition from Asia, India, Eastern Europe, Latin America, maybe even Mars.
- Nations fighting to devalue (manipulate) their currencies so their exports remain cheap and so that their citizens can keep their manufacturing jobs.
- Continued squeezing of the Middle Class.
- The proliferation of data—and access to it. (But data does not equal information and "A confused, overwhelmed mind says 'no.'")
- A never-ending, expensive fight against terrorism.
- More power given to the people as the spread of the Internet, mobile communications and social media give everyone a voice.

On the home front our new normal is:

- "Phantom" unemployment. (Just because someone runs out of unemployment doesn't mean they found a job.)
- Increased acrimony—and even violence—between our politicians and their zombie supporters.
- A sideways to negative stock market for many more years. Yes, the markets have hit plenty of new highs since Trump took office, but trees don't grow to the sky, and how will a slowdown in real estate sales impact the markets in the coming years?
- Rising interest rates after the nearly seven years of an effective Federal funds rate of 0%, which will slow down new home sales.
- Tighter credit, which contributes to the slowing of new home sales.
- Increased personal savings (a good thing for our nation in the long run but tough for

the local retailer today).

Don't Jump Off The Bridge Just Yet

Because typical, average, ordinary sales people, business owners and middle managers have their heads plugged warmly and snuggly in dark, damp places, they don't see the opportunities this "typical normal" offers anyone willing to look and act. What will it take to remain optimistic and to prosper in these times?

Be a problem solver. As economies shift, it exposes the unprepared. ("A low tide shows who's been swimming naked.") Even if you are not an expert at what needs fixing, by approaching business with your eyes wide open and optimistic about your success, you can broker relationships between the downtrodden and the professional fixers and profit handsomely for doing so.

Next, acknowledge your own weaknesses. This may require the work of a professional or the insight from a mastermind group. Hire a consultant to do an evaluation of your business, your personality traits, your marketing, your finances. Leave no stone unturned. Then outsource what you're no good at doing so you can focus 100% of your efforts on the areas where you excel.

As you dig deeper into your own business and shift your focus to being a finder of problems vs. the fixer of problems, you'll realize:

- There are a lot of messed up businesses out there.
- You ain't so bad after all.
- People will pay a lot of money to stop the pain.
- You can earn a lot of money as a business match-maker.
- You may have to stop doing something you've "always" done.
- You may have to start doing something you've always "avoided."
- Tomorrow will be a great day (unless "the creek rises and the Sun don't.")
- The Sun *will* rise tomorrow, so you better hit the ground running.
- Excuses last forever. Success takes daily, focused effort.

Welcome to the New You: Winner in the New Economy. Now take a bow. ~*~

Work Harder or Smarter?

Yes.

The successful business owners I know are up early. They are working on their businesses and themselves. They are attending conferences and workshops. They are reading and learning and listening to podcasts and books on tape. (Do they still come on tape?) They are testing new ideas, watching their competition to see what is working and what is not, and surrounding themselves with experts and motivated people that are optimistic and focused on growth and pissed off at the way the government treats entrepreneurs and business owners.

They are getting things done, they are helping people, serving the needs of the marketplace, providing jobs, feeling good about themselves and they go to bed tired, yet fulfilled, despite what the mainstream media pumps into the airwaves about the "greed" of business owners.

They realize they do have a choice in how they think and act and market and sell and grow, and they choose the hard right instead of the easy wrong.

When you are running scared, with tunnel vision, hiding from the truth and reacting to what comes your way, playing "prevent defense" instead of "aggressive offense,"—you, too, will go to bed tired but the exhaustion comes from being unfulfilled. This leads to restless nights and grumpy mornings. Soon you find yourself in a self-defeating, self-fulfilling death spiral and your business is doomed. Eventually, you have to stop allowing yourself to circle the drain and make a conscious effort to work both smarter and harder for as long as it takes, which could be many years.

Our cities, our nation, our global economy did not arrive at its current state in a month or a quarter. It will take more than a new social media account or press release or a new law from Congress to sort things out. So gird your loins, turn off the news, surround yourself with optimistic Doers and go "git 'er dun."

Now that's good advice right there. I don't care who ya are. ~✱~

The #1 Job of a Business Owner

What will a dime get you today? A radiologist (in India), a web designer (in The Philippines), a dozen bookkeepers, janitors, graphic designers, computer geeks, operations managers, HR managers, software developers, bakers and candlestick makers. That also goes for interior decorators, movers, landscape architects, caterers, therapists, counselors, carpenters and electricians.

Wanna know who's not on that list? Great marketers. Why?

Because nobody knows your business like you know your business. Nobody cares for your business like you care for your business. Your business is quite literally your child. You conceived it in your mind. You brought it to life. You were there when it belted its first, "Look at me world, I'm alive!" and when it took its first steps. You helped it through the awkward adolescence years and watched it grow into a young adult, ready to venture into the world, but still needing guidance and a knowing-ear to provide comfort and direction and maybe even protection as you both navigate turbulent waters.

A great ad man can relate, but the great ones are neither easy to find nor easy to retain. Even when you get lucky enough to

find one, or blessed enough to be able to afford one, the marketing is still your responsibility. Sure, you listen to our ideas. Sometimes you must even trust our ideas. (We are the experts, you know?) But, as a business owner, you need to keep both eyes and hands on the marketing steering wheel today, tomorrow, forever. Every day your goal is to beat yesterday's greatest ad, promotion or event.

When the phone rings with frenzied prospects that will stand in line in the rain to pay top dollar for what you're selling, you'll know you've made it.

What are you doing to keep the phone ringing and your company profiting? If you're like the average business owner I meet, not enough. But you're reading this, which means you're not average. Welcome to the above-average club where we realize that marketing is our #1 job.

As you can see, it's not lonely at the top. It's lonely at the bottom. It's lonely doing menial chores that can be outsourced for a $5 bill. It's lonely leaving the house before everyone wakes up and coming back after they're asleep. Focus on making magnetic marketing and see how lonely you're not. ~✻~

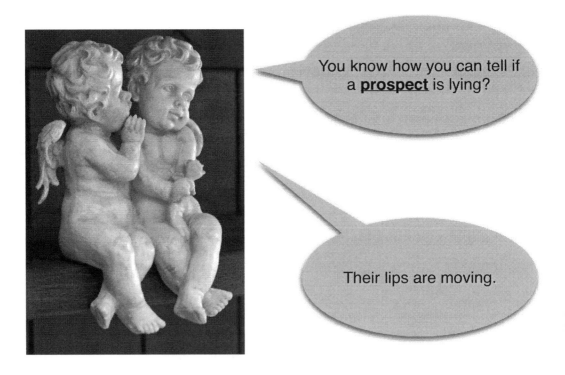

The #1 Job of a Sales Manager

The record books say the Alabama Crimson Tide won the NCAA National Championship in January 2010.

The record books are wrong.

Alabama won the January 2010 BCS Championship in February 2006 when they signed Mark Ingram Jr. to their team in the Fall of 2007. You see, in 2009 Ingram was a sophomore and was so great a player he won the first Heisman Trophy ever awarded to an Alabama player. His greatness greatly contributed to Alabama's undefeated, championship year.

The coaches at Alabama, and all great coaches, understand that to build a brighter tomorrow, you must recruit better today. The same is true for great sales managers.

Now there's a difference between "hiring" and "recruiting." NCAA Division I schools can have 85 kids on scholarship at a time but only 25 can be awarded to freshmen. So these schools must be selective in choosing those to whom they offer scholarships. However, like a plane that takes off with empty seats, it's foolish to have scholarships go unused.

Sales managers have the same dilemma. You need to let the world know you are looking for top talent and will make room for them if there is a fit. But there's a catch. (Why is there always a catch?) Back in September 2015, the Labor Force Participation rate was at 62.3%, a 37-year low. That meant there were a lot of desperate people looking for work and/or better pay, which meant more people may have been unscrupulous during the application and interview process. And by "unscrupulous" I mean they'll lie through their teeth to get a job.

(As of August 2018 it's only at 62.7%, which is well below the 66.2% back in January 2008, but the government would have us believe unemployment is low. This proves that figures can lie and liars can figure. But I digress.)

This is why you need a process to sort and sift through the hundreds of resumes you should be receiving every year in your quest to find that Heisman Trophy-caliber person for your sales team. You don't have time to talk and visit with every Tom, Dick and Harry that email you their resume.

There is good talent on the street for cheap, which means now is the time to cut your dead weight and build up your bench strength. Your people need to be thankful for a job and a paycheck and they need to work for every penny you give them. That doesn't mean you beat them with whips but it is MORE THAN FINE to expect your employees to go home tired at the end of the day.

Implementing an "always-recruiting" mentality will instill fear in your current sales staff, which will make them produce or leave on their own.

Both are good for you. As long as you are always recruiting.

Already doing that? Send me a picture of that championship trophy next year, won't ya? ~*~

The #1 Job of a Salesperson

(If you're in sales, you may want to skip this chapter. If you strive to be more than a salesperson, read and heed.)

According to Myplan.com, I made more money each year since 2001 than surgeons, anesthesiologists, OB/GYNs, oral and maxillofacial surgeons, orthodontists, radiologists, and several other medical "ists." I also topped petroleum engineers, treasurers, controllers and air traffic controllers. But that's not the really interesting part.

The interesting part is I did it while spending most of my time at home, in flip flops and a ball cap in my home office, where every day at least one of my five daughters—who have all been home-schooled—brings me coffee and snacks and hugs and kisses and my dog is asleep at my feet and my wife roams about at will.

How did I make so much money in such an easy lifestyle? By becoming effective at the #1 job of a salesperson: disqualifying people, otherwise known as prospecting.

Contrary to popular belief, the #1 job of a salesperson is not to prepare or present quotes, give presentations, haggle and overcome objections, update their CRM and company reports or sit in conference calls and sales meetings.

Their #1 job is to prospect. And the purpose of prospecting is to DISqualify, which comes as a shock to most people in sales. The old books tell us we need to qualify, pitch and press for the purchase. (That's why turnover among sales staff can exceed 30% in poorly-run organizations: poor training and even poorer expectations.)

We cannot control whether somebody reaches into their wallet and pulls out their credit card to buy what we're selling, but we can control how often we put ourselves in position to earn a sale from a qualified prospect. That is why the #1 job of a salesperson is to prospect.

Daily prospecting includes:

- Dialing the phone. (Cold calling still works. Especially in B2B.)
- Canvassing your territory door-to-door.
- Sending direct mail pieces and hand-written notes to key accounts.
- Attending industry and community events and trade shows.

- Tactically leveraging social media like LinkedIn.
- Connecting with receptionists, gate keepers and executive assistants.
- Having meaningful conversations with decision makers.
- Spending breakfast, lunch, happy hour and/or dinner with people that are not relatives and do not work for your company.
- Asking for testimonials and referrals.
- Sending targeted emails to key prospects.

What prospecting is NOT:

- Giving presentations.
- Conducting demonstrations.
- Playing on social media sites.
- Tweaking your Fantasy Football roster.
- Creating and sending proposals.
- "Sharpening your pencil."
- Answering questions. (Great salespeople ask the questions.)
- Avoiding questions.
- Completing expense reports.
- Updating your CRM.
- Playing with Photoshop or Word or creating PowerPoint presentations.
- Mailing literature to those that want you to "send over some information."

Anesthesiologists must graduate college, then a 4-year medical program, then attend four more years in an anesthesiology residency, and then possibly participate in a one year fellowship—optional but recommended. That's 13 years of advanced studies, mounting debt, errors and omissions insurance, crushing government oversight, ungodly hours and limited scotch to make a quarter of a million dollars a year.

A great salesperson can do that with no degree. No debt. No insurance. No risk of being sued by the family of people you killed doing your job. And, you can make up your mind to earn that kind of money in the next 12 months starting this very moment if you just do one thing well: prospect daily.

How badly do you want to be #1? ~✲~

How To Tell If You're About To Make a Really Bad Prospecting Call

Are you currently behind on your sales quota?

Yes

Is your boss/spouse/dad breathing down your neck?

Yes

Are you in a cubicle where everyone is listening?

Yes

Are you dialing blindly, out of sheer desperation?

Yes

Are you hungover?

Yes

No

Rock on and good on ya for actually having a backbone and picking up the phone.

You're about to make a really bad prospecting call.

(Be sure to record THAT guy. It's gonna be really bad.)

43 Year Goals
& Persistence & Commitment

The first professional football game I ever attended was with my late Uncle Jimmy in the New Orleans Superdome. The Saints, led by Archie Manning, hosted the Atlanta Falcons and, as was usually the case back then, they lost.

The year was 1979.

Uncle Jimmy had season tickets even though the Saints weren't all that good. (How's that for political correctness? The "Ain'ts," as many called them, were terrible! My, how times change.) But my uncle loved the Saints. He believed in them. He supported them. He got angry at their performances, but he never gave up on his belief that the Saints were the best.

Fast forward 43 years from their entry into the league—and 31 years from my attending that first game—and the Saints are Super Bowl Champions. Over the years their personnel changed (remember the earlier letter on recruiting?) and their playbooks changed, but their focus did not: Win the Big One!

What is Your 43-Year Goal?

Do you have a goal so big you're willing to consistently work towards it for two generations, through the scoffing and laughter of all who see you? The first step to success is having a legacy-building goal. (The second step to success is Delivering a Powerful Message in a Powerful Manner. I'll address that later in the book.)

For example, in 1967 David Dixon created plans to construct the largest fixed dome structure in the world to house his NFL expansion team. David Dixon built the largest stage in the world for a team that only existed on paper. How's that for dreaming big?

He delivered his powerful message in a powerful manner. Dixon's new team would be the best, and 31 years later he was proven correct. But he didn't do it alone. In fact, he obtained the assistance of business leaders and politicians all the way up to, and including, the Governor of Louisiana, to make his dreams come true.

If you don't have access to the governor of your state to make your dreams come true but could use a little encouragement from time to time, find and/or start a mastermind group. (You'll see this idea come up often in the book.) You may also be interested in my reassuringly-expensive 90-day private consulting that also includes lifetime access to **MakeEverySale.com**. Check out **www.WesMethod.com** to apply.

The goal of any program like mine is to hold you accountable to improve at least monthly, if not weekly. You need to improve the creation and delivery of your powerful message. You need unbiased advice (and a swift kick in the rear from time to time) and fresh perspectives and ideas on how to get closer to your 43-year goal.

Whatever you choose, get started today because 2062 will be here sooner than you think.

Happy dreaming. Happy doing. ~*~

P.S. Who says advertising is dead? Bad advertising has always been dead and good advertising has always been alive. Want proof? How many ads do people watch during the Super Bowl? I watch every one of them with my family and friends. Heck, we even rewind them so we can see them more than once.

"The real fact of the matter is that nobody reads ads. People read what interests them. Sometimes it's an ad." ~ Howard Gossage

Do you produce interesting ads? ~*~

Hey, sidebar:

Wanna know how a former Navy SEAL sets goals?

Check out the interview I did with Dan O'Shea on episode #161 of The Sales Podcast. He might be one of the fastest-talking, most-intense guests I've ever had on the show.

TheSalesWhisperer.com/session161.

Camera, ACTION!

How's this "new" economy treating you? Are you killing it yet with social media? How are those Yellow Page ads working out for ya? And billboards? And direct mail? What percentage of your clients or potential clients have their faces buried in their smartphones, tablets and laptops? How many are overwhelmed, easily-distracted, ADD with the reading comprehension of a 5th grader?

Might it be time to add video to your sales growth strategy?

Making videos used to be hard. (Sure, making great videos will always be hard. But making good-enough videos is easy and getting so easy your competition is about to start doing it to steal business from you.)

As of May 2018:
- More than 1.8 billion unique users visit YouTube each month.
- Over 6 billion hours of video are watched each month on YouTube—that's almost an hour for every person on Earth, and 50% more than last year.
- 100 hours of video are uploaded to YouTube every minute.
- 70% of YouTube traffic comes from outside the US.
- YouTube is localized in 56 countries and across 61 languages.
- According to Nielsen, YouTube reaches more US adults ages 18-34 than any cable network.
- Millions of subscriptions happen each day, and the number of people subscribing has more than doubled since last year.
  http://www.youtube.com/yt/press/statistics.html

To make videos "back in the day," i.e. 2006, you needed:
- Two Apple computers—MacBook Air and 27" iMac ($3,100+).
- Video software ($99 to $299).
- HD Cameras (Samsung HD—$159, Kodak Zi-8—$209; Nikon D5200 DSLR—$1,200).
- Olympus stereo microphone—$49.
- Tripods—standard and Joby Gorillapod ($79 and $22).
- Hosted video software—$250/yr.
- Flash conversion software—free to $347.
- Online hosting—Amazon S3—cheap to use, took me a month to learn and become proficient.
- Premium hosted program for creating, converting, storing, embedding and submitting video to the top 20 video sites—$3,000/yr.

Now you can get a Logitech HD webcam for $70 at Sam's Club and record straight to YouTube where you can also edit, annotate and monetize for free.

Adding video to business profiles:

- Increases number of business profile views more than 100%
- Increases number of profile clicks more than 30%
- Increases number of calls generated by more than 18%
- Video drives a wide range of customer actions:
- Increases number of visits to advertiser sites by 55%
- Increases physical store visits by 30%
- Increases incidence of purchase by 24%

Video on social media sites can drive more traffic to your site. Video on your website can inform and convert more visitors to prospects. Video on your website can inform and convert more prospects to clients. Video for your clients can educate, upsell, and retain current clients.

Even average, moderately-decent video will help you beat your competition that is too fat, dumb or lazy to leverage video. Example: of the video results for the phrase "short sale san diego experts" on 10/5/13, the top video was made on 5/5/09 and none were made in 2013! If you change the phrase to be "san diego short sale expert" there is only one video made this entire year, and it's the 10th result in Google.

If you're shy, do instructional video screencasts with programs like Camtasia (PCs and Macs) or Screenflow ($99 on a Mac). Camtasia is owned by TechSmith and offers Jing for free. However, your recording time is limited, and they include a watermark, but it's a great tool to   get started.

And getting started is key. Failure-to-launch is the #1 cause of failure in business. Period.

The #2 cause of failure is being invisible. Your potential clients are looking for video. So what are you waiting for? The world wants to see your video.

Action! ~*~

Disciplined Optimism

"If you're not growing you're dying." ~Tony Robbins (among others)

"Sell or die." ~Me (among others)

Life is a game and to succeed you must compete.

As a young man playing football in high school and college, I was the quiet one in the corner before the game reviewing my roles and responsibilities, thinking through the plays, studying the opponent and envisioning how I would do all that I could to take away their will to compete as soon as the whistle blew.

At the same time, there were always a few guys who would hoop and holler and run around high-fiving everyone, slapping them on the backside to get us all "psyched-up." (Interestingly, these were the same guys that hung their heads low as soon as any adversity arose such as the opponent making a big gain or scoring early, or someone getting hurt. It was then I realized hype and optimism are extrinsic, they are shallow and they are fleeting.)

Playing on a team meant I couldn't get away from the "feel-gooders." Today, I can, and I do, put quite a bit of distance between myself and these New Age Positive-Thinking-Vision-Board-Crazy-Happies.

Don't get me wrong. I'm not some "glass-is-half-empty" kind of guy thinking the sky is falling.

Quite the contrary. Things are great behind the pages of your book. They have never been better, and the future has never looked brighter. Why? Disciplined Optimism.

I got that phrase back in 2010 from Chapter 5 of the book "Conquer the Chaos," written by Infusionsoft founders Clate Mask and Scott Martineau. Disciplined Optimism is like being "cautiously optimistic" or "planning for the worst, but preparing for the best." It gives you the strength and fortitude to persevere and stick with the game plan despite high highs and low lows.

In Conquer the Chaos, Clate and Scott refer to the Stockdale Paradox, a name given to Admiral James Stockdale by Jim Collins, author of "Good to Great." Stockdale spent seven years as a prisoner of war during Vietnam and won a Medal of Honor for his efforts resisting the North Vietnamese Communists.

As Collins was interviewing Stockdale he asked him who were the P.O.W.s that didn't make it home from the Hanoi Hilton. "Oh, that's easy," said Stockdale, "the optimists. Oh, they were the ones who said, 'We're going to be out by Christmas.' And Christmas would come, and Christmas would go. Then they'd say, 'We're going to be out by Easter.' And Easter would come, and Easter would go. And then Thanksgiving, and then it would be Christmas again. And they died of a broken heart."

Stockdale concluded with, "This is a very important lesson. You must never confuse faith that you will prevail in the end—which you can never afford to lose—with the discipline to confront the most brutal facts of your current reality, whatever they might be" (Collins 2001, 84-86) (Mask, Martineau, 2010, 81-81).

What brutal facts have you been ignoring?

Are sales down? Are sales cycles increasing, along with your competition? Are your salespeople making more excuses than appointments? Are you not generating enough traffic to your website and converting enough leads from your website, trade shows, ads, etc? Are you wasting money on marketing that is not producing a measurable, positive ROI? Are you tolerating mediocrity, complacency and excuses from those around you? From yourself?

Contrary to what my good friend Dione Moser at Impact Marketing will tell you, I'm not a pessimist. I just call 'em like I see 'em as a "disciplined optimist." That's why I have more money in the bank today than the day I left a 6-figure sales job in Corporate America despite having more kids, opening an office, and tripling my staff since then.

You can prevail if you focus on your current reality while maintaining the faith of a child in a prosperous outcome.

What are you focused on today? ~*~

Daily Success vs. Lifetime Excuses

Sam's dad was an Ohio tanner. (For you city slickers, that means his dad took animal skins and turned them into leather.) It's rather hard work *today*, let alone 185 years ago. Suffice it to say, Sam was raised as what the politically correct would call "working class." (**Excuse 1**)

At the age of 17, Sam got into college but they got his name wrong. When he tried to change it, they told him to either live by the wrong name in college or go home with his true name. (**Excuse 2**)

Sam was middle-of-the road in college. (**Excuse 3**) But he excelled as a horseman. Upon graduation, Sam joined the Army but instead of being placed—logically—into the cavalry, he was ordered to work in supplies and logistics (yawn!). (**Excuse 4**) After a relatively-successful 11-year career where he actually saw a little action on the front lines, he got sideways with a superior officer and was forced to resign immediately despite having a wife and two children to support. (**Excuse 5**)

For seven years he struggled as a farmer, a bill collector and endured another failed business, only to end up, at the age of 38, working as an assistant to his dad. (A whole lotta good that college degree did him!) (**Excuse 6**) Then war broke out. (**Excuse 7**)

(THIS IS WHERE IT WOULD HAVE BEEN EXPECTED AND UNDERSTANDABLE IF SAM HAD GONE ON A DRINKING BINGE AND KILLED HIMSELF. I MEAN, COME ON! HE HAD 7 KILLER EXCUSES TO QUIT, RIGHT? RIGHT?)

But Sam loved his country and fought for Her. In fact, he fought so well he was made Commanding General of the United States Army in less than three years. Four years later he was elected President of the United States. Four years thence he was reelected President of the United States.

"Sam" was the nickname Hiram Ulysses Grant was given by his West Point classmates after Thomas Hamer, the Congressman who appointed Grant to West Point, forgot Hiram was his first name. (Wow, a politician making a mistake!? Good thing our government outlawed mistakes.) Hamer knew that Simpson was Grant's mother's maiden name and mistakenly assumed Simpson was Ulysses Grant's middle name. Therefore, Hamer filled out the application in the name of "Ulysses S. Grant."

So when "Lyss" showed up at West Point, his classmates took the initials of U.S. from "Uncle Sam" and applied it to U.S. Grant, ergo, "Sam."
Sam got back up every time he was knocked down, right up to the day he died. Sam persevered. Perseverance takes effort. All great achievements come from the consistent application of effort. Apply the effort.

Let us know if we can help. ~✶~

Marketing From Outer Space

Hello, my creative friend. When was the last time you received an email from the moon? Or a post card from the sun? Or a letter from a Space Shuttle? Don't try thinking about it. You'd remember it if you did!

Guess what? So would your clients. That's why I recommend you take a fresh look at Google and play with their Maps. When you get there, type in "Wilson Green Manor Temecula, CA."

There should be a red pin of sorts on the location. If you double click right next to it, the map will zoom in. Keep clicking until you see the shadows of the mansion. (Make sure "Satellite" is checked in the bottom left.) You can tell the image was shot in the summer around noon because the shadows are all cast to the top/north of the building but they are short. (Yes, I'm a weather geek.)

Over on the top left under the search bar and image, next to the name "Wilson Creek Manor," and their reviews you'll see "Direction." Click that. In the new navigation screen on the top left the name and address of the venue will be pre-filled in as the destination while the top row will be blank. Enter "San Diego International Airport" and click "Enter."

You'll see that it's 67.9 miles. Why is that important? I'll tell you later.

Now imagine your best client or top prospect worked in downtown San Diego, CA and you wanted to invite them to The Sales Whisperer® worldwide headquarters or Wilson Creek Manor for a 2-day intensive mastermind/workshop you were conducting. How cool would it be if you printed the directions from their office to your meeting location and mailed it to them with an astronaut stamp and a letter like this:

"Dear Prospect:

"We're so excited that you will be attending our workshop. Your bank account will most surely be enriched, while your brain will be enlivened. To be sure you know exactly where to go, I have enclosed directions straight from the San Diego International Airport to the seminar. What a thrill it will be to see you blah, blah, blah, blah, blah…"

Suppose you're in the real estate industry and you're actually a DOER and you sent this letter and photo to a prospect:

"Dear Listing Prospect,

"Enclosed are directions from your house to a comparable house in your neighborhood that I sold last month after just 38 days for $775,400. After 12 years serving the housing needs of this community, I know that your home has more upgrades, a larger lot and a better view than the home enclosed. With that in mind, I believe I can help you sell your home for more money and in less time yada, yada, yada…"

I know what you're thinking…

"**But, Wes! My business is DIFFERENT!** I sell computers and the technology industry is soooooo cutthroat and we're just viewed as a commodity!"

Try this one, my right brain-oriented Chicken Little:

"Dear CIO,

"Enclosed please find a satellite photo of the exact facility here IN AMERICA that manufactures the finest blade servers in the world. If you look two buildings to the west (792 yards away by foot) you'll see the location of the support facility that will take your calls, coordinate your installations, and provide the best support of any technology company on the planet. Yip, yip, yahoo!"

Might they remember these letters? Probably. Will you have the guts to try it? You'll FOR SURE make money if you do.

Now back to those San Diego International Airport to Temecula, CA directions:

Nestled just an hour's drive from the San Diego airport, in the heart of the Temecula Valley Wine Country, is the home of The Sales Whisperer® where—at least several times per year—some type of live sales and marketing training is conducted to help professional salespeople, sales managers, business owners and entrepreneurs sell more, faster, at a higher margin, with less stress and more fun.

When we meet, we eat and drink like kings and queens while staying up well past our normal bedtimes because your mind is set free, the limitations are removed, and your path is made clear, maybe for the first time ever. Sometimes we awaken the giant within—albeit with a bit of a headache in the morning—but with a spring in our steps.

But you need to get here for the transformation to begin. San Diego is easy to fly into. The weather here is always nice. The beer is always cold. The wine is always local (as well as the beer and even some of the spirits!) And the marketing we'll help you create will be out of this world.

Now go plan your trip. You are coming to our next gig, right?
~✱~

P.S. After you make plans to come see me, have fun touring the globe for a few minutes, then make plans to finally visit the places you've put off for lack of time and/or money because you will eliminate those issues after we meet. Having the time and the means to take my family of nine to Hawaii for nine days and to travel with my oldest son for 6-9 days in San Francisco, Argentina, India, and the U.K. as he completes his studies in the first graduating class of Minerva® Schools at KGI—www.Minerva.kgi.edu—I can tell you the time, money, and effort you invest to get good at sales, marketing, and systems is worth it.

It's a big world. It's a small world. It's yours for the taking. I'll help you put a big "X" to mark your marketing spot.

Striving To Collect...Aluminum Cans?

It's 5:25 a.m. Saturday morning and I'm at my MacBook, typing away, which is not unusual. What's unusual is what is on my mind this morning because of the dream I had last night.

In this dream, I came home and a friend of ours was visiting with my wife and they were standing in the kitchen. Our friend had one of those plastic bags you get at the grocery store and she was collecting our empty aluminum cans and in the dream, it hit me rather hard.

Here's this elegant woman I know from church, and times are so hard she is collecting our aluminum cans for extra money. It was such a huge shock because I thought she and her husband were doing fine. Obviously, looks can be deceiving.

Then a few things dawned on me, besides the morning sun:
- I was mad that they let things go for so long that they had to resort to collecting cans to make ends meet.
- I was happy that they were rolling up their sleeves to do what they had to do to make ends meet.
- I was honored that they were willing to "let their hair down" and come to my wife and me to help them reach their goals.

In my blurry, harried, adventurous 48+ years, I have stepped in more than my fair share of heaping, steaming piles of dung, many of which I created on my own. I have made and lost a lot money and friends along the way. I have lost more sleep than a mother nursing a newborn and I have done the happy dance at some of the deals I have structured and the resulting checks, some so big I almost blush thinking about them.

Through it all, I have found a few constants in my life that give me the courage to hop out of bed each day and produce.

1. **The love of my family.** My wife, my parents, my sister, my cousins are all happy to see me whether I'm rolling up in my BMW or my old mini-van with a transmission that leaks on their driveway.

2. **The support of my friends.** Going

through tough times helps you learn who your friends are and they, too, are just happy to see you. Some have even LITERALLY given me the shirt off of their backs. (But those are stories best told bellied up to a bar with a cold drink in our hands!)

3. **The love of God.** He does not change nor does His love. Being a father of seven, I now understand the story of the Prodigal Son. My oldest two are boys and they do some boneheaded things from time to time. Even though they can get under my skin, my love for them only grows. While I may not be happy with their particular course of action at any given moment, I still love them, and, regardless of what they do, if they sincerely apologize and seek to make amends for their transgressions, they are welcomed back (I'll write more on TOUGH LOVE in another chapter.)

4. **The inevitable success of motion over meditation.** There are days (and sometimes weeks) when I feel like I'm not getting anything done, when I feel like I'm wasting time or chasing a pipe dream or I've bitten off more than I can chew. There are times when I've missed my goal or fallen behind on a project and I feel like crawling back into bed and saying "To hell with it all! What's the point?" Then it happens. A small victory appears. A prospect from 6 months ago calls out of the blue and says, "We're ready to buy." Then it happens again. A client calls you with a HUGE referral that closes immediately. Then it happens yet again. A prime office space opens up that's twice the size and half the rent, enabling you to expand and grow at no extra expense. In football, they teach running backs to keep their legs and feet moving because good things happen when you have the ball and you're moving straight ahead, eyes on the goal, teeth clenched, pummeling your opponent, determined to cross the finish line NO MATTER HOW MANY TIMES YOU GET KNOCKED DOWN! Sometimes you're tackled, but you only need one good run out of four in football to be a success. Besides, it's those steady, consistent runs up the middle for 1 and 2 and 3 yard gains that wear down the defense, which makes the 75-yard run for the win possible. And that 75-yard run is all they'll show on ESPN! So keep moving.

Today, celebrate your family, your friends and the love of God and commit to taking massive, consistent action to surpass your goals and live your dreams.

When's the last time you called an old friend just to say hi? Or hung out with your family doing whatever they wanted? Or went to Church? Go do them all now.

.ₐₛ$$$$$$$$$$$$$$$$$$$$ₛₛₛₛₛ

The next chapter will wait for you. After you've done all of the above and you think you need some help with your business like Sally did, you know how to find me…~✶

The Power of "S"

"The only real security that a man can have in this world is a reserve of knowledge, experience and ability." ~ Henry Ford

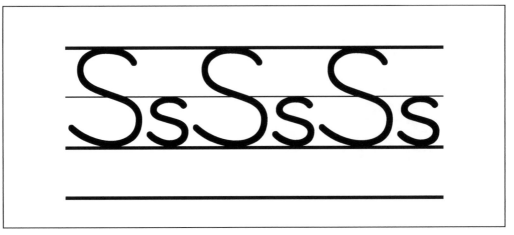

If you were arrested on charges of being a 21st century marketer would there be enough evidence to convict you? Can your prospective clients find you easily? Do you provide resources to educate and disqualify the tire-kickers and attract the best prospects to you?

For Example:
The poster child for the smoking, cratering disaster formerly known as the real estate bubble is California. (The house we rented from 12/04 to 2/10 went from $189 per square foot to $66 at auction. OUCH!) However, investors with cash have never stopped scooping up properties like they're giant Tootsie Rolls falling out of a great mortgage piñata in the sky! That proves there is always money out there but you need to shift your marketing and attitude to correspond with the realities of the marketplace in order to get your **unfair** share of the shifting real estate pie.

How are realtors adapting to this shifting market? Turning to Google, I did a simple search for "short sale realtors" and discovered a mere 9,040,000 results. Since I don't have the time to sort through 9 million results, I narrowed my search to "san diego short sale experts." This helped—611,000 results—but still too many for anyone besides a government employee to weed through.

Because I don't need an army of experts, I chopped the "s" off of my search and did an <u>exact phrase search</u> for "san diego short sale expert." By removing that one little letter, realtors that specialize in short sales in the San Diego area have an 85% better chance of being found—76,400 vs. 499,000 results.

In reality though, 75,399 competitors are still too many, but these two little tips—learned and applied in under five minutes —will give you a 99.8% better chance to beat your competition. Think you can discover, learn and execute with precision the 100 or 1,000 other little tips like this you need to grow on your own? How large is your reserve of knowledge, experience and ability?

It's only lonely at the top if you choose to be alone. To grow quickly, seek the counsel of experts, surround yourself with knowledgeable, experienced, able professionals and you'll always be at the top, which means you'll never be lonely. ~*~

Hey, sidebar:

It's the details that matter.

In The Make Every Sale Community I cover every component of the sale from cold calls to voicemails to befriending assistants and receptionists to setting firm appointments.

We also get into building the correct multi-step, multi-media sales, marketing, and nurturing campaigns for your business that run both before and after the sale.

This is where the attention to detail comes into play. You see, most businesses and salespeople say things like

"We've helped a lot of people in a lot ways for a lot of years, which is why you should call us and give us all of your money."

How convincing is that compared to

"In the last 10.5 years I've helped 2,355 business owners in 28 countries increase inbound leads an average of 303% within 90 days without adding additional staff."

Get more details and specifics from your clients then use them in your marketing.

If you do that I guarantee you'll quickly turn "Ss" into "$$ $s."

Clowns Aren't The BEST Jugglers

entrepreneur: en-tre-pre-neur: [ahn-truh-pruh-nur] noun

Etymology: French, from Old French, from entreprendre to undertake: one who organizes, manages, and assumes the risks of a business or enterprise (According to Merriam-Webster)

Juggling clowns are exactly like entrepreneurs, with one teeny, tiny exception: JUGGLERS TRAIN RIGOROUSLY, ARDUOUSLY AND IN A FOCUSED MANNER FOR YEARS to perfect the trade before jumping on stage.

We entrepreneurs afflicted by "restless mind syndrome," which is brought on by...

- Being subjected to bosses who can't sell but are given divisions—and even entire companies—to run.
- Getting laid off three times in two years (twice on your birthday) and five times in five years.
- Being forced to sell a product that is not ready "or else," (the threat from the boss that can't sell).
- Verbal abuse from the boss that can't sell.
- Being forced to travel on Mother's Day and Valentine's Day and skip an annual retreat all in the same year.

...just hop right in and start our own ventures because we get fed up with the inefficiencies, the lack of respect, the lure of more money and control over our lives. More times than not, we're not really prepared for life and business on our own.

This happens because Entrepreneurs are doers. We don't read the manuals. That's what "managers" and "technicians" are for. We get things done, or at least we get them started! We're the dreamers, the big picture people, the visionaries. Then we quickly become the losers-of-sleep and the anxious as we realize how many things must be managed, maintained and massaged just to keep the business going, let alone growing.

We soon find ourselves wishing we had read the owner's manual, but "How To Succeed at Entrepreneurship: The Starter's Guide" hasn't been written. So, it's trial by fire.

Sure, sure, there are nice people in the government that want to help but then "over-help." The SBA website has a Small Business Planner section with a 4-step, 31-part, 522-section guide on their homepage to help you "Manage your business from start to finish." (I wish I was kidding.) Heck, I made it through 5 years of college and two degrees without reading and writing as many reports as the SBA recommends!

But wait. There's more! To show you just how thorough the good ol' SBA is, they'll help you fail! (If I'm lying I'm dying!) According to Step 4, Part 30 they help you file for bankruptcy! How's that for thorough help? How can you plan for success AND failure at the same time?

You and I both know the typical dreamer, go-to-gal, doer, mover, shaker, producer is not ever, not once, gonna even visit the SBA website, let alone read all the way down to Step 4 with its 31 glorious parts. And we sure as heck aren't going to write an 87-page business plan with 178 footnotes, 45 charts, a table of contents and an appendix along with a 5-year earnings projection and ROI calculations. (How close are all of those forecasts on those business plans created back in 2008?)

Nope. We just jump right in and "figure it out as we go." Soon, we discover that the road to the top or right under a bus is determined by the way we manage three key lists:

- "To-Do"
- "Still-To-Do"
- "When-Will-It-Ever-Get-Done?"

So we juggle on a tightrope, without a net, in front of a live studio audience all day, every day until we do figure it out.

Congratulations on possessing the spirit that made this country great, and know that you are not alone.

Know that failure is not a person, it is an event.

Know that now is the time to do what your competition is either unwilling or unable to do and it will pay off for you sooner rather than later.

Know that you deserve success and you deserve the best.

Know that making money is not dirty or evil, nor is it anything to be ashamed of.

Know that God really and truly only gives you what you can handle.
And know that you did make a decision to drain the swamp, and we all know that

alligators live in swamps. So don't be surprised when you're up to your neck in alligators.

That's when you'll know it's time to make some boots, belts, and purses, then pull out the deep fryer because fried alligator, when done right, really does taste like chicken.

While Keith may not cook up much alligator here in SoCal, he has cooked up a winning formula for growing his sales… ~*~

> "We have had the busiest March since we started our business over 20 years ago. Tuesday of this week we had to park cars on the public street because I didn't have any room on our lot. I just finished measuring our gross sales of March 1-27
>
> "Our sales are up 27% over the previous year.
>
> "We can point to many reasons for this (a slightly improved economy, better consumer confidence etc). But I can tell you a growing number of First Time Customers have come in telling me they found our shop by searching the internet. Since I haven't done much on my end to increase our internet exposure I must give the credit to Wes at The Sales Whisperer. Thanks Wes for doing such a great job!!"
>
> **Keith Greene, Owner**
> **Old Town Tire & Service**

Beep! Beep!

.₁₅$$$$$$$$$$$$$$$$$$ₛₛₛₛ.

Social—Anti-Profit—Media

I closed my Facebook account and it was a glorious time.

Like many, I got caught up in the social media whirlwind and let it consume me rather than serve me. So I converted my Profile to a Page and merged it with my existing Page for The Sales Whisperer® and enjoyed the silence.

What I didn't know was how often people were screaming "Where are you?" into the social media void I had created. People were freaking out. They thought I was hurt or sick or didn't like them or was angry with them. (In reality, I was angry with a few "friends" that are too "out there" in their zealotry for how we should eat, vote, raise our kids, etc., so I've kept them hidden from my life.) But during that time of no Facebook I was amazed at how addicted I had become to checking my social media accounts, and how productive I could be without it.

Sure, there are some benefits to being active on social media. I do interact with a couple of great groups for sales and marketing, and I do get some good feedback from those that like my page, but "COME ON, MAN!" For most of us, social media is a drug. It's a distraction. It's a way to see if old lovers still look good or have let themselves go. To talk smack about politics or sports. To stay in touch with family and friends in faraway places. To do anything but work.

Hence the name: SOCIAL media.

It's a place to be social (and more anti-social, actually.)

There's a time and place to be social. It's just not while you're working. If your business success depends on your efficiency and leadership, cut back on the time you spend on social media, and watch your profits and income soar.

Don't worry. Invitations to play Candy Crush (I can't believe that's still a thing) and to connect with high school sweethearts and to read celebrity gossip and see pictures of dogs and cats and babies wearing sunglasses and to connect with "@no_real_life is going to have a cheese sandwich and take a nap" will all be there patiently awaiting your less-frequent check-in.

Social Media and Social Marketing *may* help you grow. However, like any new medium and skill, there are tips, tricks, techniques and tools that must be mastered if you are to control it. Otherwise, it will consume and control you either through wasting time trying to figure it out on your own or by losing to those that already have or to those that have the wisdom and self-control to focus their energies elsewhere, on ventures that provide a better, proven ROI.

Is your goal to be social or to be profitable? ~*~

> "You are practical, patient, no nonsense, and have an amazing ability to get to the heart of the matter. In developing a strategy for building my audience, we didn't have a clue about what we were doing. As a direct result of working with Wes, I began to *see* what pieces of my marketing strategy needed to be put into place; and most importantly, in what order!
>
> "I'd been trying to follow the advice of a lot of online marketers, but I was driving myself crazy implementing things that for which I simply wasn't prepared to follow through.
>
> "We recommend you to anyone who...is serious about building a solid foundation for their business."
>
> Sally Rubin
> Park Rubin Media

Superiority

In the Gospel of John we are told that the truth will set us free.

Today the truth is setting many weak businesses run by good people, and good businesses run by weak people, free of running their businesses at all.

The truth behind the truth is that consumers "vote" with their wallets and as they become more discerning with their spending, SUPERIOR MARKETERS are rewarded with a larger share of that *walleted*-vote. Being a superior "doer" of what you do is not enough. To be a superior marketer, you must be comfortable thinking of yourself, your product and your service as worthy of superior pricing and then you must be comfortable telling the world this fact.

This is harder than it sounds because over a generation we have been force-fed such drivel and nonsense as "outcome-based-education" and "non-competitive" sporting leagues where they don't keep score. (In May 2009, I attended a game in Chicago played by the young daughter of a classmate of mine and the parents were not allowed to cheer! I kid you not. They didn't want to create "too much pressure or hostility with exuberant applause and support." You can't make this stuff up.)

But the marketplace keeps score.
Your prospects keep score.
Your clients keep score.

"But, Wes, How do I become a tooter of my own horn? How do I become comfortable developing and sending superior marketing that sets me apart from the competition, that builds value in the mind of my prospect and gives me the right to charge premium pricing while my competition grovels for crumbs and negotiates on such erudite items as free shipping and engraving?"

Several ways:

1. Retain someone that has superior knowledge or expertise in a particular field in which you need to improve. (Outsource your weaknesses.)

2. Be open to review by your peers and ignore the fence-sitters, the by-standers, & the peanut gallery that only live to critique the PRODUCERS.

3. Find someone that has produced superior results of their own AND ARE STILL DOING IT. I say "still doing it" because our marketplace, nation, and world have changed dramatically since 2008 and are still changing before our very eyes. Marketing and sales tools and techniques that made money in 2007 may be pooh pooh today.

4. Seek out "devil's advocates." If your idea or program can't stand up to a little scrutiny by a fellow expert with a different viewpoint, how tough are you and how good is your plan? Really. Tough times call for tough people taking tough action. Now sit up straight and take it like a pro. Remember, it's just business and steel sharpens steel.

5. Listen to well-meaning friends and family IF they have no agenda, no axe to grind and are close to the ideal profile of your prospects. Otherwise, ignore their "advice."

You can choose to toot your own horn.
You can choose to develop yourself.
You can choose to celebrate and embrace your superiority.
You can choose to make more money in any economy.
The choice is yours.
But choose you must.

Remember, Life is good. It's *gooder* when you're selling. ~*~

11 Things We Can All Agree On At Thanksgiving

Enjoy this Thanksgiving blog post from 2012. It's funny any time of year.

After that, please squeeze a loved one tight. Eat a little extra dessert. Hang out an extra 15 minutes with your sweetie. Tickle a baby's neck and chuckle while they giggle and you'll know there's a lot to be thankful for all year long.

Happy Living.

After this extended, acrimonious election cycle, isn't it great to know there are things we can all agree on at Thanksgiving?

1. Those little turkeys our kids make out of pine cones at school are still cool! (So are the turkeys they make out of paper plates.)

2. Speaking of paper plates, kids under 18 should ONLY eat Thanksgiving off of paper plates (with those little plastic support thingies under them.)

3. It's OK to let Fido eat "people food" this one day. (And baby can eat dog food!)
4. Joggers that run on Thanksgiving day are just showing off.
5. Grandpa WILL fall asleep on the couch. (Grandma probably will, too.)

6. The TV CANNOT get loud enough for Grandpa. (And closed captions don't help, because he can't see that far.)

7. The kids will want to play in the same room the family is watching the game.

8. We all have a relative that requires us to put "the good Scotch" in a hidden location.

9. Someone will spill something on something else you wish they hadn't.

10. You'll be told the next day that one of your visitors has a fever and is throwing up!

11.The day will go by too fast.

Happy Thanksgiving from The Sales Whisperer® family to yours.
We have a lot to be thankful for.

May God bless you, your family, and the United States of
America. ~☆~

The $250,000 Script

Cue the whiny, tinny, violin music...

"A script?! Wes, I can't follow a script! It doesn't feel natural. I know what I'm doing. I don't want to come across as salesy or cheesy or pushy. I've been in this business since Burger King was just a Prince! (Besides, only rookies need scripts.)"

(Can you hear the music? This is where Lassie gets shot!)

What if you could grow your bottom line by $250,000 by following a short, simple, natural script or two that would take maybe 30 minutes to learn?

(Can you hear the music? This is when help is on the way and you realize Lassie is going to live!)

In 2009, I received a call from a gentlemen three time zones away asking if I could help him grow his family's preschool. After some in-depth discussions over the course of about a month, we reached an agreement to work together for at least 90 days on a host of issues to grow their business.

In a nutshell we:
• Converted their website to Wordpress so they could update it easily.
• Created a great free report for lead capture.
• Installed a web form to automate the correspondence with new leads.
• Created a follow-up sequence for new leads.
• Gathered about 10 video testimonials we put on YouTube and embedded on their site to help drive traffic and give visitors a warm and fuzzy.
• Optimized their site's SEO—Search Engine Optimization—to help them appear in search engines for their keywords.
• And another half dozen or so little things to help prospects both find and feel comfortable with the preschool.

Results after the first month:
• The site was popping up nicely on Google.
• Leads were up about 150%.
• But revenue hadn't increased.

Results after the second month:
• The site was still popping up nicely on Google.
• Leads were still up about 150%.
• Leads converted to tours was up over 200%.

- But revenue hadn't increased much.

Results after the third month:
- The site was still popping up nicely on Google.
- Leads were still up about 150%.
- Leads converted to tours was up over 30%.
- Tours converted to new enrollments were up nearly 400% (from 9% to almost 35%).

Final Figures: The preschool was full after 87 days and their bottom line revenue grew $250,000 over the subsequent 12 months.

They, like most companies, didn't have a traffic problem. They had a conversion problem. The biggest change we made that contributed to their dramatic growth was scripting out the words they and their staff used when:
- Answering the phone.
- Scheduling tours.
- Conducting tours.
- Securing enrollments at the conclusion of the tour before the prospect "escaped" home to "think it over."

Sure, it helped to have more "at bats" by increasing the number of leads, but it didn't increase their revenue. Remember, they had a conversion problem, not a traffic problem.

So before you go nuts trying to grow traffic, pay attention to the words you use when you interact with your current visitors. I'll bet a dollar to a donut you are leaving money on the table by not focusing on what you say and how you say it to those that are already interested in what you offer.

Once you maximize your conversions, you'll have the funds you need for all that other fancy-pants stuff you keep reading about and think you have to do.

That is, if you still need it.

Is that your phone ringing? What are you going to say when you answer it? ~✶~

Hey, sidebar:

You may be thinking *"There are too many potentialities. Too many variables for me to be able to create a script for every engagement and interaction with all of my prospects. Besides, I'm good at what I do so I'll just go with the flow."*

If you're thinking this, you're not alone. I thought the same thing back in my over-working, under-performing selling days but I was young and hungry and had the time and energy to go with the flow.

It was also before social media took over, high speed wireless data reached the four corners of the globe, and bots driven by artificial intelligence started taking over our web searches, our browsing history, our communications, and even our thermostats!

But despite all the changes, our human brains and how they become engaged and disengaged has not changed in thousands of years and not even Zuckerberg can change that.

You see, the busier, more distracted, more harried we get the more important it is to follow a script because the people with whom we are engaging are more predictable than ever. They're unprepared for a real, meaningful dialogue so when you show up with intention, with purpose, with a plan that includes a proven script, you, too, will add $250,000 to your bottom line—or more.

~~The End~~. The Beginning.

The Power of 1%

Selling like you did just 22 months ago won't cut it in today's environment.

If you ignore that statement you'll be worse off financially 22 months from now.

Bold statement? Yes.
True statement? You know deep down it is.

What can you do about it?
Take Massive Action by taking 100 Tiny Actions.

Allow me to explain with a golf story. Between April 5-8, 2007 in Augusta, GA, the #1 golfer in the world, Tiger Woods, was playing a pretty good game. "Pretty good" meant that it only took him 291 strokes to complete four rounds at the most prestigious golf course in the world. However, the winner, Zach Johnson, took only 289. So Tiger lost by a measly two strokes after four days of sweat, concentration and effort, not counting the four practice days leading up to the tournament.

If Tiger was just 0.687% better he would have tied for first and forced a playoff. If he was just 1.03% better over four days—or 0.26% better each day—he would've won outright. Tiger would have taken home 241% more money if he was just 0.26% better each day for 4 days! Not 10% better. Not 5% better. Not even 1% better each day. He just had to be 1% better in total to take home an extra $763,667. So for each of his three missed putts or errant drives or missed greens he lost $254,555.67.

Before you start to feel too sad for Tiger, please realize he has it pretty good because in professional golf, those that "hang on" and play on the weekend, get paid *something*.

Imagine if the world of sales worked that way? "Wes, Your computer system is almost as good as the top vendor so we'll still pay you something because you made a good run at it"? AURGH?!

When you and I lose a bid or a contract we get ZIP, ZERO, NADA, GOOSE-EGGS, NOTHING! The good news is you and I have at least 100 things we can improve in our business just 1% that will put us at the top of our game. A few of them are difficult but together they are life-altering and could put an extra $700,000 in your pocket, if not this year then certainly over your sales career.

This constant, steady improvement is not an option. Consumers have less discretionary income today, and that will continue to be the case for years to come. The buying habits of consumers have changed for a generation.

You can take control of the situation by becoming diligent, demanding and critical of every process in your business and sales cycle to squeeze every ounce of excellence out of each of them. Nothing is too small or unimportant to escape critique. Here is just a partial list of what you can improve just 1% in your business quite easily:

- Business cards—are you using both sides of the card with a call to action?
- Email signature—include links to your social media profiles and a P.S. to a free report to increase connections and opt-ins.
- Logo—not life or death for a small business, but does it need refreshing? Does it pack a punch or sit there like soggy celery?
- Voicemail greeting—are you aloof or friendly? Change it every month or even every week to inform callers about your promotions or new releases.
- Company literature—is it all "Me. Me. Me." or does it speak to the client's needs?
- Website—is it a "brochure" website or is it interactive with an educational component as well as a lead-capture feature?

You can always install pop-up software for cheap to capture leads if it's too hard to change your site.

- Blog—are you creating fresh content at least once a week?
- Social Media—is it mastering you or are you mastering it?
- SEO—do you know what it means or have you buried your head in the sand? Your site needs to be labeled correctly so search engines can bring hungry prospects with money to you. Why do this? In February 2013 I took in $36,268.12 with no salespeople, no full time employees, no paid advertising and no outbound calls, because my SEO is solid.
- Testimonials / Video testimonials—are you asking for them from every client? All smartphones now create video in HD and you can host it for free on YouTube. Visit www.thesaleswhisperer.com/fans/ for examples.
- Promptness—do you let your people wander into the office any time they want? Show up for meetings late? Turn in sales forecasts and reports late? Lead by example and raise your level of expectation of everyone.

It's not as daunting as you think to get started. In 30 days you'll see great improvements, significant improvements. In 60 days and in 90 days, you won't recognize your own business. It all starts with you making up your mind to no longer accept "good enough." Once you apply a critical eye to your business you'll find areas to improve.

Do you want a blind eye that leads to a black eye or do you have the guts to take a fresh look at your business with eyes wide open? Here's looking at you, Kid. ~*~

Celebrities & Drugs. Salespeople & Hugs.

Why do celebrities do drugs and why do salespeople need hugs? Because they have a poor self-image and low self-esteem.

I won't get into why I think celebrities have such poor self-images (and I do have my opinions I'd be glad to share over an adult beverage if you're ever in SoCal), but I will share my ideas on why sales people in general, and new sales people in particular, have such low self-esteem.

One word: Confusion.

In 100% of the companies that bring me in, their sales management skills are 180° out of whack! Low morale, high sales staff turnover, eroding margins, excessive cancellations and customer complaints are typical because sales managers manage RESULTS instead of ACTIVITY.

What does that mean?

Without a gun, you and I cannot control what our clients and prospects do. We cannot MAKE THEM reach for their checkbook and open it up to us. But we can control whether or not we called them and asked for an appointment and asked pertinent, relevant, thought-provoking questions that showed our expertise and competence.

But every company I've ever worked at, as either an employee or consultant, manages results instead of activity. (In a way I'm glad because this means they need me.) This style of management leads to "hockey stick" sales results. You know those that all come at the end of the month at lower margins and higher stress?

The way you build a great sales organization is to manage activity and pay on results. When that new sales person shows up, they should be told something along the lines of:
- Your quota is $12,000/month, which is $3,000/week.
- The average sale is $1,000, which means you need to land three new clients a week.
- The average closing ratio is 33%, which means you need 3 appointments to make a sale, which means you need 9 appointments a week.
- Since 25% of your appointment will cancel you need to make 4 appointments to get 3, which means you need to set at least 12 appointments a week.

- To get one appointment, you must speak to 5 decision makers and follow this exact script, so you must speak to at least 60 decision makers a week.
- To reach 5 decision makers, you must speak to 20 gatekeepers and follow this exact script.
- To reach 20 gatekeepers, you must make between 35-50 calls a day and follow this exact script, and...
- Go to three networking events a week and deliver this exact USP, and...
- Give two talks a week on this topic to this audience with this exact call to action, and...
- Mail 50 pieces of attention-getting marketing pieces a week to these exact businesses with this exact call to action, and...

You get the point. And you know you're not doing it this way.

Most of the time the sales manager will say something like, "You're a big boy. You've been in this game long enough. You know what to do. I'm not going to hold your hand. I hired you for your industry experience and tenacity. Now go sell something!" They then proceed back into their office with their "open door policy" because you're all "family."

If there is new-hire "sales training," it's more like "product training" where they are briefed on all of the patents your company owns, the model numbers and dimensions of the gizmos you manufacture, your number of employees and offices around the world and how the founder started the company in her garage. The new hires are then handed some brochures or shown where to download them on the company intranet, slapped on the back and told "to go make sales." (How's that working out fer ya?)

This is the beginning of the end for that sales rep and they just started! Their excitement quickly turns to confusion and dejection because they see others making sales at the company but they're not sure how to start, what to say and more importantly, what questions to ask. But they know how many employees you have and how to navigate the company intranet.

Now do you see why sales people need hugs?

How well do you know the minimum activity numbers for sales success at your company? What's the exact process your sales people must follow every day to hit their numbers? What kind of example are you setting for your sales staff? This is why I made No More Sales Duds, **www.NoMoreSalesDuds.com**. You may also want to enroll in The Make Every Sale Community at **www.MakeEverySale.com**.

Consider them my virtual hug for motivated sales leaders. ~*~

What's Acceptable Soon Becomes Inevitable

We live in dangerous, trying, demanding, chaotic, anxious times full of strife, anger, hostility…and love, and generosity, and hope, and opportunity.

August 9, 2012 marked the 5-year anniversary since the housing / financial crisis tried to choke the life out of the world. U.S. unemployment was between 8.3% and 25%, depending on which side of the aisle you sit. (People who stop looking for work are still unemployed, but I digress.) Obama and Romney campaigned so nastily it made Caligula blush. HP cut 27,000 jobs. Microsoft announced its first ever quarterly loss.

Gloom and death and destruction are everywhere, right? RIGHT? Then why is Keith Greene having his best year ever at Old Town Tire and Service? Jill Morris, co-owner of Hampden Twp.'s Central Pennsylvania Academy of Gymnastics is killing it…"I'd say we're probably 80% full for all our classes, which puts us a month ahead of where we usually are. And we're looking at being 110 or 120 % of capacity when registrations end, so we've gone ahead and added classes and hired three new staff members." (Blog.pennlive.com)

By Frits Ahlefeldt

Tom (my nephew) and Kassandra just began a new, hope-filled, optimistic lifelong journey full of love and encouragement, smiles and kisses. And dozens of entrepreneurs purchased coaching programs that run as much as $12,000 this weekend to surround themselves with fellow dreamers, planners and doers to ensure their tomorrow is brighter, fuller, livelier and more profitable than today.

Examples of Optimism Personified

A "retired" school teacher (forced to retire by the kind, loving, tolerant Orange County school district she selflessly served for 27 years) plunked down $13,495 for her daughter to get the best entrepreneurial coaching on the planet because she believed in her.

A single mom committed to a $149/mo coaching program to learn how to market her writings skills and services. She knew if she walked out of that 3-day conference without believing enough in herself that she would learn and do what it takes to make that money back in spades, she wouldn't do anything once the Monday morning alarm clock clanged.

A newly-wed, aspiring vegan chef—who works crazy full time+ hours in another line of work (to hide from making time for her passion) — not only made money by selling her own creations for the first time ever, she sold her muffins and recipes for an amount higher than she expected. This happened Friday and Saturday after I helped her Thursday night break through a HUGE issue she had about money, which was engrained in her soul from watching her father struggle financially.

Sidebar: Discussing money is just as "dirty" as talking about sex, politics and religion. (And people wonder why most businesses fail!?) Money is just a convenient representation of the value you give to society. Anyone that tells you "money is the root of all evil" is a lying manipulator, ignorant bastard or both. 1 Timothy 6:10 says "THE LOVE OF MONEY IS THE ROOT OF ALL EVIL." If you teach the former quote from now on there is a special place in Hell for you. Consider yourself warned. (End of Sidebar.)

Everyone in the workshop that weekend realized that the habits, the excuses, the fears, the worries, the ignorance of business principles, the poor work habits, the poor investing habits, the poor sales and marketing skills had led to the creation of their undesirable lifestyle.

What are you tolerating in your life?
• Low pay, maybe even a recent pay cut

- Sleazy competitors
- Downward price competition
- Sloppy vendors
- Lazy employees
- Rude bosses
- Slow paying clients
- Unresponsive contractors
- Belittling friends
- Down-in-the-mouth friends?

If you accept any or all of the above, they will soon become inevitable in your life. As soon as you become proactive and intentional in your personal life, business life, prayer life, etc. good things will start to happen.

Professional training and mentoring can cure your sales and marketing evils. Cure your sales and marketing evils and you'll make more money. Make more money and you'll cure your business woes. Cure your business woes and you'll have a better outlook on life. Have a better, more optimistic outlook on life and you'll begin curing your sales evils and marketing evils. (It' the Circle of Sales.)

Feelings don't follow actions. Taking action creates the positive feelings.

How are you feeling now? What are you going to do anyway? ~*~

Social Media Marketing and Unicorns and Rainbows

You can wish or work to make money. But "hope" is not a strategy.

"If you've read about social media, or been to any marketing conferences, you've probably heard tons of advice like love your customers, engage in the conversation, be yourself, and make friends. I call this unicorns-and-rainbows advice. Take a couple of time-honored adages, add in the unquestioning awe of an unaware audience, and pretty soon you've got an entire industry based on easy-to-agree-with but unsubstantiated ideas. But there's a problem. Myths aren't real and superstitions often do more harm than good."
~Dan Zarrella , Zarrella's Hierarchy of Contagiousness

So many people think "if I just get a Twitter account and Facebook Fan Page I can grow my business." The irony is most people are neither sociable or knowledgeable when it comes to marketing but when it comes to Twotting and Facetubing and YouBooking, somehow two wrongs make a right.

Ask yourself this: How persuasive, powerful, influential and interesting am I? If the answer is somewhere between "not very" and "kind of," you're just spinning your wheels and self-medicating as you goof off (that's what you're really doing) on your social media accounts.

If you want to grow you need to focus on the message, not the medium. To focus on the message you need to focus on the "Who" and then it will become much easier to focus on the message. Since you can't sell or service everyone, you need to choose who to lose. There is power in stating what you are not, what you won't stand for, what you leave out, i.e. gluten-free, Zero Calories and Non-GMO. Once you are clear on this, shout it out loud and proud.

Until you get a backbone of steel and tell the world what you stand for and what you don't and deliver this powerful message in a powerful manner, you'd be better off waiting for Santa Claus to bring you that golden list of buyers. At least you wouldn't get sucked into worthless debates on Facebook and Twitter and get depressed reading the average comment on YouTube. (I mean, really.)

To grow you need to work smart and hard,

make the 1% improvements in every aspect of your business, take massive action and leverage the best tools to Attract, Bond, Convert, Dazzle and Endear (ABCDE) your clients.
My secret weapon is at www.BuyCRMNow.com. What's yours? ~*~

Hey, sidebar:

This may be hard to believe but you do realize that you are the product when it comes to social media platforms, right? If you get a product for free, your attention, your browsing patterns, your shopping patterns, the free information you provide about yourself via the cute quizzes you answer every day like "What kind of vegetable are you?" or "What's your hotness level?" are all vital pieces of information advertisers—and Russians and politicians—use on a daily basis to manipulate, persuade, and convince you of things and to do things you may not want to be thinking or doing.

Additionally, most businesses have no business being on social media for three primary reasons:
1. You're not social
2. You don't understand the media
3. Because of #2 you're using it incorrectly.

Jay Baer is a New York Times best selling author, sought-after speaker, and successful marketing consultant. Way back on episode #15 of The Sales Podcast he said *"Social media is not a great customer acquisition tool…It's more of a loyalty and retention play. You never go to Facebook and like some company you never heard of."*

Later on he dropped this **bombshell:**
"If you're not great at email, you have no business doing social media. If you can't send out one great thing a week or build a nurturing sequence inside (your marketing automation platform), why would you want to tackle something that happens in real time?"

Listen to Jay Baer's interview at
**www.TheSalesWhisperer.com/
session15**.

Get the help you need overcoming 1, 2, and 3 in The Make Every Sale Community at
www.MakeEverySale.com.

Communication Celebration (Word Up, Wordpress)

Back in the day, only the wealthy could read because books were expensive. They were expensive because they were all written by hand and took a long time to create. Along came Gutenberg in 1440 with the printing press and communication and education got easier. But dang, type-setting and refilling those ink drums was a pain!

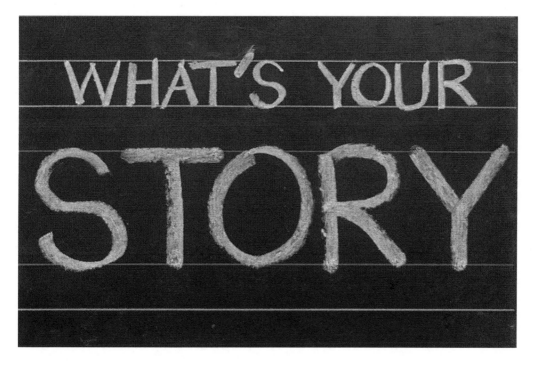

Fast forward 540 years. Senator Al Gore invents the internet and communication explodes again. But, Dang-Dang! Who wants to learn HTML or pay a web guy $50 to $100 per hour and wait 3-6 weeks every time you want to make a change on your website?

Zoom forward 23 years and Matt Mullenweg brings us Wordpress.com to power web logs or "blogs" fast, free and easy. (If you can create a Word file or slide presentation or spreadsheet, you can launch a Wordpress blog.)

Hop, skip and jump ahead 7 years (Moore's Law says processing power doubles every 2 years, so 7 years is a lot!) and the line between web sites and blogs has blurred to the point of *undetectabilityness*. (Is that a word? Look it up on a free internet tool, Google, which will direct you to another free tool, Wikipedia or Dictionary.com. Do you see the trend? Your potential clients are looking for free education—and entertainment, preferable via *video—to make an informed decision. Are you providing that education or are you leaving that up to your competitors?)

So what's holding you back from getting your message out to the masses? Despite what the dunderheads and slothfull-of-thinking want you to believe, content is still king. People will read what interests them, even if it's your ad, as long as you write something interesting.

The best time to plant a tree—or start a blog—is 20 years ago. The next best time is today.

Welcome to your potentially-well-communicated world. What do you have to say for yourself? ~*~

*Hey, a sorta sidebar:

Yes, video is important in your sales and marketing efforts, but so is the printed word, i.e. not on-screen digital words.

Naomi S. Baron, an American University linguist who studies digital communication of "those dang meddling kids," and the author of "Words Onscreen: The Fate of Reading in a Digital World," explains in her book the science of why printed books are often better than digital books. In a nutshell, we tend to skim when we read on screens and when you add in the increased distraction, which is inevitable, our comprehension suffers.

Over the many years of her work, Baron's favorite response to the question of what students liked least about reading printed books: "It takes me longer because I read more carefully."

So if even millennials and post-millennials prefer tangible books, won't your prospects and clients as well?

Now go print something.

The Profitability of Convenience

The only reason to be in business is to make a profit.

Yeah, yeah. Maybe you want to "do good" and "make the world a better place" and "serve the under-privileged," etc., but even non-profits need to grow their donations so they can stay around long enough to actually make a dent in the universe.

A sure way to grow your profits is to make it easy for people to give you their money. For example, your grocery store places *The National Enquirer* and *Cosmopolitan* and sodas and M&M'S® at the checkout line on purpose. (And it's not an accident that the candy is down low where your kids can see it and beg for it.) Few of us go to the grocery store and stand in line just for *People* magazine. But if we like the cover story and we're already spending $50 or $100 or $200, what's another $3 in candy or $7 in magazines? (By the way, a $7 sale on top of $50 is a 14% increase. It's 3.5% of $200.)

What would it be worth to your bottom line if you grew sales 3.5-14% just by rearranging your actual or virtual storefront and shopping cart and gave your customers a chance to spend more money with you easily?

Grocery stores also have those little shelves so you can write a check. They've turned the credit card machine around so you can quickly swipe your own card and they have automatic change dispensers that speed you along and reduce mistakes. You can learn a lot from your weekly grocery run if you care to look. *"But, Wes. I have an online business and I don't sell magazines. Come on, man!!"*

You're right. What was I thinking? Henry Ford must've been a fool to get inspiration for his car ASSEMBLY line from a meat-packing DISASSEMBLY line. Those two had nothing in common. And Gutenberg was a fool to look at wine presses and metal stamping machines for his inspiration to invent the printing press. Those two had nothing in common.

Wow.

My apologies. I must be off my game today

Please put down this book (created with no help from Gutenberg) and hop in your automobile (created with no help from Ford) and head on over to your local grocer with your kids to pick up your favorite treat...but make sure that's all you buy because you're too savvy and sophisticated to fall for those sales and marketing "gambits," right? ~*~

Hey, sidebar:

This may sound like it's right from the Department of the Obvious but make it easy and convenient for your prospects to pay you.

Yes, American Express charges higher fees so raise your prices 5% or 25% or 125% to make up for it. Think that can't be successfully done practically overnight? Read Alycia's testimonial below.

Yes, PayPal can be a pain in the butt with their silly reporting. But people like using it.

Yes, taking checks can slow things down but on bigger deals I'm happy to take checks. It eliminates the merchant account fees and guess what: your customers can't file a chargeback on a check.

So accept as many forms of payment as you can so it's easy for your prospects and customers to pay you and repay you.

If you need help raising your prices, hit me up.

www.TheSalesWhisperer.com/contact

> *"Wes, you showed me how to grow my leads 383% in our first month, 337% the second month, raise my prices 2x-10x, and grow my paid subscribers 54% all within 90 days."*
>
> **Alycia Wicker**
> **www.AlyciaWicker.com**

The Profitability of Timing

The only reason to be in business is to make a profit. (Didn't I just say that?)

To grow your profits, you must present relevant offers at the moment of relevancy. Why do you think Google places "sponsored" ads on the top and along the right of every search? THAT is how they make money: presenting relevant options to "shoppers"—you and me—at the moment of relevance.

We type in "iPhone" and we see ads from Apple, Sprint, Samsung (to compete), Best Buy, Target, Avobuy.com, Best Discounts, Motorola (another competitor looking to persuade) and Amazon.

Google gets paid when we click on one of those ads. (Notice there are no ads for motorcycles or plastic surgery or Rottweilers or juggling clowns. Those are not relevant to the search "iPhone.")

How relevant and timely are your offers?

If you sell cars, you should offer specials on tune ups, oil changes and tire rotations. If you own a restaurant, your offers could include catering, group event specials or "dinner for four." (Everyone does "dinner for two," so why not double your sales with the same amount of ink?)

To make relevant offers you need to master the art of list-building. You need to know your clientele so you don't send steak dinner offers to your vegetarian subscribers or remodeling coupons to renters.

To make relevant offers, you need to master the art of timing. Just as it is in sports, music and comedy, timing is everything in sales. You must make a relevant offer at the moment of relevancy. If you are too slow in making your, offer you'll learn that "time kills deals." (Own a restaurant? Consider showing the dessert tray as you take the dinner order so your patrons leave room for dessert.)

If you are too fast, you'll appear pushy, desperate or both. (You don't immediately push for a $4,000 Mac sale to someone that comes in to look at $200 iPods...but you could ask if they would like to see the iPad Mini or even the full size iPad. That's a relevant, timely offer.)

There is nothing wrong with subtle "trial closes" early in the sales process because sometimes people know what they want and are ready to buy but they may want or need you to ask for their business. But if your normal sales cycle requires time and due diligence on the part of your buyers, give them that time as you make them aware of your full range of relevant offerings.

This is harder than it sounds but it's worth the effort. Why do you think Amazon shows "Customers who viewed this also viewed"?

Now go make a relevant sale. ~*~

Hey, sidebar:

Along the lines of timing, having the discipline, forethought, and guts to ask the hard questions at the right time—i.e., earlier in the relationship—is fundamental to sales success.

Nathan is a go-getter in The Make Every Sale Community. He calls on medical clinics to help them get more cash patients and he's hungry to grow, but he's new in this field so he's making a few mistakes. Just last night he was posting questions in our private group about how and when he should send over the Sales Agenda that will guide their meeting today.

He's been in the group long enough to understand the importance of having a mutually-agreed upon agenda for the key meeting with the decision makers, but he's still new enough that in the process of applying everything else he has learned to get his foot in the door, he forgot to review the Sales Agenda so he was asking if he should send it via email so they'd have it in their inbox when they got to the office.

The problem with doing it that way is that there is no agreement with the meeting attendees so I recommended he email it to them just before the meeting and open with a review of it and ask if everyone agrees to what is outlined.

By opening this way he is letting the prospects know that he has a plan, that this isn't his first rodeo, and that he is not there to do a song and dance while providing free education and entertainment for them.

You can control your sales meetings with **TheSalesAgenda.com**.

The Profitability of One-Time Offers

The only reason to be in business is to make a profit. (Am I making myself clear?)

To grow your profits, leverage the fear of loss we all have by making a fantastic offer to a new prospect or customer the moment they identify themselves. Think about it. You've done the heavy lifting in that you...

- Designed, paid for and ran ads for your business to get people to visit your site or come into your store or pick up the phone and call.
- Worked on SEO so your site would appear on the first page of Google, Bing, Yahoo! for your ideal keywords.
- Created a killer "lead magnet" and tied it to an auto-responder so visitors to your site would opt-in, thereby identifying themselves to you as warm prospects looking for what you do and interested in how you say you do it and trusting you enough to give you their contact information...

But everyone is distracted and has ADHD and is chasing shiny objects so you need to do something FAST to snap them out of their distracted state and get them to focus on buying from you. You may take website and storefront visitors for granted, but you have created no small amount of momentum in getting them to come to you. Now boost your profits 10%-100%-1,000% by presenting GREAT one-time-offers to both prospects and clients to get them to either reach for their wallet for the first time or add to the purchase they just made.

Examples of one-time-offers include:
- A pop-up that offers 10% off and appears when visitors try to leave your site without buying.
- An "Add To Cart" upsell offer that gives buyers free shipping if they add a second unit to their order.
- An email or postcard sent a week after their first purchase that says "Use this coupon to take 20% off your next order" with a short expiration date.

This is why restaurants have "specials of the day," Sam's Club has "Roadshows," and Amazon offers free shipping on orders of $25 or more. You need to order that seafood, buy that sofa or add another item now or lose that offer forever.

Now go make one-time-offers 100 or 1,000 times this week and let me know how much more money you made. (Feel free to send me some. I'm not too proud to take tips. :-) ~☆~

Hey, sidebar:

Do you know what items have the largest margins for fast food chains like McDonald's? The drinks like sodas and coffee.

They lure you in with a special on their sandwiches and make it up when you add fries, a soda, and/or a dessert to your order.

In session 78 of The Sales Podcast—**TheSalesPodcast.com/ session78**—with Andrea Waltz we discussed why you should "Go For No."

She and her husband learned this when they were in the eyewear sales business and his manager asked him if he had offered a new customer various upsell items such as a second pair, sunglasses, anti-glare, custom cases, etc.

You can package these as simple offers that compliment the purchase or at a discount if bundled together.

The point is simple: people who buy a baseball glove will probably buy a batting glove, ball, bat, cleats, caps, sunscreen, maybe even a DVD series on how to play baseball, so offer it to them.

You know what else they might buy? Chiropractic or massage services, fitness training, a gym membership, protein powder, vitamins, and other supplements, so have referral agreements in place with experts in those fields and help your customers partake of those related offers when they're in a buying frame of mind.

Or keep cold-calling and making one-off sales of hamburgers at 20% margins while your friends are selling sodas at 500% margins.

The Reason To Make a Sale

Making a sale is exciting, but it can be tiring and exhausting because "you're only as good as your last sale." And every month, quarter and year you're back at zero.

But it doesn't have to be that way.

When you set out to make a sale, do you get a list of ideal prospects so you can make a one-time sale or do you sell something to build a great list of future prospects?

"Isn't this a chicken and egg thing, Wes?"

Yes and no.

Have you ever wondered how those "As Seen On TV" products are sold so cheaply? The businesses behind those promotions are building a list of people that buy things on TV so they can then sell those people similar items at higher prices over and over and over. (They also sell the contact information of the buyers and make even more money.)

Savvy entrepreneurs make a sale to build a list of buyers because they know it's much easier and profitable to make a repeat sale than it is to make the original sale. Once they have a buyer, they find similar or complimentary offerings to present, thereby ensuring they always have someone to talk to, they know what to say when they talk to them, and they never start the month at zero.

Recognizing this model is the key to changing your business, your income and your life forever.

For example, if you work for a nursery, get a list of new home buyers and/or associate with real estate agents, pool companies, electricians, plumbers, and carpenters, offer them a referral fee for anyone they send to you that buys. And ask for the same from them.

That way, when you are meeting with a new client that just bought a truckload of Acacia Salacinas or Photinias you can ask them about their remodeling plans, which could open the door for you to introduce your associates in the other trades and generate a nice commission on something you don't have to carry or service while endearing yourself to the client that now views you as a trusted resource for more than just plants. As an added bonus, your referral partner's sense of "reciprocity" will kick in, which will make them feel obligated to return the favor by sending you a referral sooner rather than later.

Another way to approach this is to go through your list of past clients that purchased trees more than two years ago, and offer a tree-trimming service or custom bird-houses from your local carpenter or hummingbird feeders from your local hardware store or a raised garden built by your local handyman or even your own company.

Once you begin approaching your business this way, you'll realize the opportunities for upsells, cross-sells, referrals and expansion are literally endless.

To maintain margins and your sanity, approach every sale with the third sale in mind and let me know how you view your business 90 days from now. Will you do that for me? ~✶~

Selling To Dead People (They Don't Just Vote, Ya Know?)

"But, Wes, MY business is different. I can only make one sale to my client and that's it."

Really? Let's look at the casket-selling industry. Can't get much tougher than trying to make repeat sales to dead people, right? First of all, making assumptions is a bad thing in sales because ALL buyers of caskets are ALIVE when they buy them, either for themselves or a loved one.

For the sake of this discussion, let's say the buyer is a woman making pre-need arrangements for herself and her husband. She comes in and buys a nice set of matching mahogany caskets with matching lace, silk and satin and arranges a payment plan with the salesman. To hone in on this buyer, let's say she's 65 years old, she and her husband just retired, they're upper-middle class and love Wayne Newton.

What else might a 65-year old, upper-middle class couple add to their pre-arrangement purchase? Since they're buying caskets, maybe they'd buy a $10,000 or $50,000 burial policy to make sure they are not a "burden" on their children. You know those policies you see on TV and in Reader's Digest that require no physical exam?

Cha-ching.

Now that they have invested for the funeral, you could offer them a private family plot at a nice savings if they commit today.

Cha-ching.

Maybe they could use a referral to a good estate-planning attorney. With the current stock market gyrations, might they also need a new financial advisor? Maybe they need a good real estate agent to help them downsize or move into an active adult community. Maybe they need a new travel agent to help them see the world like they've dreamed of doing together for 40 years.

Does the funeral home offer estate planning or financial advice or travel help? Probably not.

Can they create a mastermind group of people in those fields and send them referrals for either a referral fee or reciprocal business that helps everyone in their group because they are addressing ALL of the needs of their clients?

Yes.

Cha-ching, cha-ching, cha-ching!

Having clients in the funeral home / cemetery industry, I know for a fact the new and different items they offer as up-sells are tremendous and needed and purchased and are adding to the bottom lines of the more creative companies that realize they must differentiate or suffocate.

How do YOU differentiate and add onto YOUR typical sale?

What are you offering your new prospects and clients to get them spending more, faster with you? It's the same as when you're asked to super-size your order or add a hot apple pie for just 99¢ or you're given Sirius satellite free for 3 months with your new car.

Figure out what your new clients and prospects will buy from you IMMEDIATELY upon raising their hands and/or pulling out their wallets to make their initial purchase and you'll have more happy clients and more money in your bank account.

Now go make your competitors plan their "Going Six Feet Under " sale. ~*~

The Best Time To Change

The year is 1991.
Iraq learns how we treat bullies.
Bush 41 is winding down his presidency (he just didn't know it yet.)
The Dow tops 3,000.
The New York Giants hand the Buffalo Bills the first of their four consecutive Super Bowl losses.

Meanwhile, Joe, the spritely, ostentatious college senior 970 miles from home with a quick wit and a sharp tongue (that earned him nearly as many demerits as lifelong friends) is preparing to enter "the real world."

He is ready to break free of the cocoon of academia with its yells and bells, tests and ties, invocations and expectations, introspections and inspections, all of which were certified and verified by individuals best described as managers instead of leaders (which is why Joe earned so many demerits, but that's the subject of another Whisper.)

On November 19, 1991, David also tells the world he's ready. For 15 years he has been preparing for this day. It was a "reinvention" of himself and his band and it took guts because despite achieving "superstar" status more than four years prior, David was not afraid to push himself and his band to change, to do what he felt was right, what he knew he needed to do.

The result? Paul David Hewson, aka "Bono," has sold over 150 million albums (are they still called albums?) and won more Grammys—22—than any other band in the world. (And you're trying to tell me you can't change? How many records do you want to set?)

David and his band are not alone in not being satisfied with "just being on top" or "now that I'm on top I'll just coast because everyone knows me and it's too much effort to make big changes for incremental gains."

After winning the Masters by 12 shots in 1997 as a rookie, Tiger Woods also made a change. He changed his swing despite winning the most prestigious golf tournament in the world as a young man barely old enough to drink. The result? He accelerated his pace to become the winningest golfer in history. (Then his personal life got in the way, but I digress.)

Think those are isolated stories? McDonald's® now sells more chicken than Kentucky Fried Chicken® since introducing the McNugget in 1982. Del Taco® now sells hamburgers and Microsoft® is getting into the hardware and tablet business. (Ignore that last example. But you get the point.)

The great ones put more pressure on themselves to excel and improve and grow than the outside world ever will. That's why they are the great ones! Jack Welch once said something along the lines of, *If the change on the outside is greater than the change on the inside, the end is near.*

The great ones know that nothing detects weakness like a little —or A LOT—of pressure. That is why the great ones continuously reinvent ways to test and strain and push themselves and their systems beyond what they expect to see in the "real world" so they are sure they can not only handle whatever may come their way but they can seize it and capitalize on it to their advantage.

Right now, we're finding out not only which of our competitors are weak but where we, ourselves, could improve as well. What are you discovering about your business, your processes, your products, your people, your marketing, your selling during these pressure-packed days?

When it comes to your success, are you a catalyst for change and continuous improvement, or are you a bottleneck? When it comes to your marketplace, are your prospects not visiting you because they don't know about you...or because they do? How do you know? Of the big deals you won in the last 6 months, why did you win them? Of the big deals you lost in the last 6 months, why did you lose them?

(Funny and sad sidebar: when I ask sales people these questions, they answer the former with "Because I'm good" and they answer the latter with, "Because our product stinks!" or "Our pricing is too high!" or "We didn't have it in stock!," etc., but it's never "I lost the sale because of something I did or didn't do.")

If you're a Superstar today, take a moment to pat yourself on the back then commit to yourself to do whatever it takes to be a Superstar tomorrow. If you're not a Superstar today, take comfort in the fact that few of them will take my advice in the previous sentence, which means Superstar status is within your reach, but you gotta reach.

Ready. Set. Change. ~✸~

Wingmen and The Not-So-Lone Ranger

A wingman is defined as a pilot who supports another in a potentially dangerous flying environment. It's different from a co-pilot, in that you and the wingman are each in control of your own aircraft. In other words, you're your own boss. You're in control of your own destiny. You have a mission to accomplish but you are not alone.

During my 4 years at USAFA—especially the "Doolie" or "SMACK*" year—and 5 years on active duty, this concept was hammered home daily, if not hourly, because in the profession of arms in general, and that of the combat pilot in particular, the chances of completing the mission and returning home for a cold one increase dramatically when you have a competent wingman watching your back.

"But, Wes, I'm a John Wayne, Rambo, Superman fan. The really tough guys all work alone."

Sure, Rambo and James Bond worked alone, but they A) have troubled pasts and B) are fictional characters. Heck, even the Lone Ranger has Tonto.

In business, the historical Titans like Carnegie, Rockefeller and J.P. Morgan turned to one another to conquer a political threat during the 1900 election, (where they bought Teddy's presidency). Jack Welch, of General Electric fame, turned to Dr. Ram Charan. Steve Jobs had Larry Ellison, Ken Segall and many others (he was a tormented soul). And Bill Gates had Steve Ballmer.

So if you think having a trusted advisor/partner/mentor around to help you navigate the potholes and crevasses of business makes you weak, you are weaker and more exposed than you realize. (Please keep reading.)

It's only lonely at the top if you allow it to be. Now's the time to build a great team, surround yourself with excellence, take massive action and let the world know you are ready for success. But you need someone to watch your back.

Because only our moms have eyes in the back of their heads, right? ~*~

*SMACK—Soldier Minus Ability, Coordination, Knowledge. It's not a fun year. But you learn what you're made of and it's a year nobody can ever take away from a military academy cadet that makes it through.

Are You Satisfied With "Normal"?

"Normal is getting dressed in clothes that you buy for work and driving through traffic in a car that you are still paying for—in order to get to the job you need to pay for the clothes and the car, and the house you leave vacant all day so you can afford to live in it." ~**Ellen Goodman**

Allow me to get all "Scriptural" on you for a moment to let you know that God brought you into this world to live abundantly, to make a difference.

- **In Isaiah 48:17** He says, "I am the Lord your God who teaches you to profit."
- **Job 36:11** says, "If they obey and serve Him, they shall spend their days in prosperity,..."
- **Duet 8:18** tells us, "He gives you the ability to produce wealth..."

So let me ask you something: Are you a Producer or Consumer of wealth?

Do you get up 30 minutes before your co-workers—and your competition—with a plan for the day and start improving your life and the lives of your family by delivering a product or service of value, that is needed by your community?

Or do you hit the snooze 5 times, drag your butt into work tired and late (and hungover?) only to spend 24 minutes drinking coffee, complaining of traffic, discussing the game as you keep anyone within earshot from getting any work done themselves only to plop down at your desk 24 minutes after your 13-minute late arrival so you can check a few emails, roll your eyes at the report you're behind on, tell your co-workers how stupid your clients are and how stupid management is because you don't have any good leads, then spend 7.5 more hours shirking responsibility, jumping to conclusions and stabbing everyone in the back so you can go home with nothing accomplished and wonder why you're so tired and disgruntled and in debt only to bury the wonderment in a bottle of self-medication that "helps you sleep"?

If you're the "30-minute-early type" read on. If the latter describes you...you would not have read this far, so read on, also...If you're working hard, not cutting corners, doing what you're "supposed to be doing," ask yourself: are you just doing what every other "normal" person in your position does or are you working differently?

It's simple to live that life of prosperity and abundance God wants you to live by doing just one thing: Stop Being Normal.

Normal is boring, uninteresting and it's a recipe for failure in anything you do. Normal barbers get $2 tips. Normal waitresses earn 15%. Normal business books sell less than 5,000 copies. (THANK YOU for buying this book.)

The equation of "**normal = forgettable = sure failure**" applies in spades to marketing your business. If you're not sure what normal marketing is in your industry, just look at what your competitors are doing...then do the opposite.

If your ad looks, sounds and says the same thing as everyone else in your industry, the only way the consumer can differentiate you is by your price. And unless you're Wal-Mart®, it doesn't pay to be the low-cost provider.

So tell a story. Make an impression. Capture the attention of the consumers in your marketplace and do not apologize for what you do, how you do it and for whom it is you do it.

In other words, "choose who to lose." Since we cannot be all things to all people, be proud to be a business owner and stand for something. Maybe you're a restaurant that only buys locally or only uses organic ingredients or serves the largest portions. Maybe you support the NRA in your barbershop or the DNC in your nail salon. Hang posters of the respective organizations proudly in your place of business and show FoxNews in your barbershop and MSNBC in your nail salon and tell anyone that complains to get the hell out.

That'll cause a stir, which is word of mouth, which is what you need to build a memorable, lasting, abnormal business.
Do you want to be considered "abnormal?"

Since being broke, depressed and in debt is normal, choose to be abnormal. Or is it non-normal? Or un-normal? Or anti-normal?

Be any or all of them. Just don't be normal. Deal? ~✭~

My oldest and me in Patagonia about to hike up to Mount Fitz Roy, May 2017. (He made it, I didn't!)

The Non-Normal Sales Professional

Sales Success Tip #19: Seek to serve. A sale may be the solution.

In my live training, I write a word on a piece of paper and turn it face down then ask the audience to tell me what comes to mind when I say the word "salesman."

Without fail, the word "pushy" comes out by the 2nd or 3rd word. (And this is in a roomful of salespeople, business owners and entrepreneurs.) So if those in the profession of sales think of it as a "pushy" job, is it any wonder people react with horror and angst if you ask "Are you in sales?"

The irony is that great salespeople make more money than most attorneys and even anesthesiologists. Because they are great salespeople, they come across as neither pushy nor *salesy*, which is why they make so much money. (Funny how that works, ain't it?)

Would you like to act—and earn—like a non-normal salesman? It starts at the beginning, which is your attitude. Are you in sales to serve or are you in sales to make money? If it's the latter, you'll make decent money for awhile but you'll hop from job to job leaving a wake of burned clients, employers and co-workers on your way to becoming a thrice-divorced, ladies-night-attending, gold-chain-wearing, chesthair-showing, convertible-driving, purple-pill-popping, 58-year old surfer with a pot belly hanging out with college coeds that are naive enough to listen to your stories, as long as you're buying. Or you could end up in upper-middle management at IBM, although the two are not mutually-exclusive.

If you're in sales to serve your fellow citizen by providing value in the form of effective products and services at reasonable prices, you'll make all the money you want to make. (And it's great to make your acquaintance. Welcome to the club.) This approach to the profession of sales—and the fact we treat selling as a profession—is the #1 reason we are #1 in what we do and the #1 reason we are non-normal. (I don't want to call us "abnormal," but I have been called worse.)

The profits of the selling profession follow the attitude of service. It comes from knowing not everyone is your prospect—you DISqualify—and that the only thing you can truly control is your attitude and your daily activities. We cannot control if someone will do business with us, but you knew that already.

If you're curious how non-normal sales people act, turn the page. ~✱~

How To Act Like a Non-Normal Salesperson

Non-normal sales people know that every little, teeny, tiny, itty, bitty thing they do, matters. This applies to the words that come out of your mouth when you welcome a customer to your business, speak to an executive assistant on the phone, greet a prospect at a trade show, hand out your business card at a Chamber of Commerce networking event or craft an email newsletter, Yellow Pages ad or radio spot for your local talk radio station.

To become interesting—even intriguing—start at the beginning. Literally look at how you engage your prospects in the first 3-7 seconds of every interaction you have with them: on the phone, via email, in person. If you have influence over your company's marketing, this applies to your advertising as well.

So just how good *are* your opening statements, your elevator pitches, your Unique Selling Proposition (USP), your Unique Value Proposition (UVP) and your headlines? Would you like some examples to get the juices flowing?

- "This will make you feel like you're 16 years old again—but with better judgment." (Health supplement, energy drink, vitamins, exercise CD, gym membership, etc.)
- "There are two types of people in the world... those who get an extra paycheck in their mailbox every week, and those who don't." (Investment services, direct marketing business opportunities)
- "This will make your skin feel like you're 16 years old, but without the acne." (Skin care, health supplement, spa treatment, facial treatment)
- "How would you like to get a check every time your neighbor picks up the phone?" (Cellular plans, text plans, phone service)
- "I show people how to fire their boss." (Sales training, investment services)
- "Get the 3 secrets your boss doesn't want you to know." (Franchise sales, personal development programs)
- "Do you know why your job is making you poor?" (Mix and match any from above.)
- "I show people how to laugh at morning commuters from the comfort of your bed." (Ditto)

Non-Normal salespeople understand that their job is to disqualify everyone they meet by tossing out fabulous openers and seeing who takes the bait. This approach has the added benefit of eliminating rejection, which is the #1 reason salespeople do not prospect. If all you're doing is throwing out strong USPs and opening lines and expecting the person to ignore the opening, you can then simply enjoy the company of those that don't take the bait and play hard-to-get with those that do.

You play hard-to-get by asking great questions of those that express interest, because whomever is asking the questions is in charge of the conversation. This is done by asking great followup questions rather than telling them everything you do and how you do it. For example, if I tell someone, "I'm an expert at helping businesses automate their marketing and sales" and they ask, "Really, how do you do that?" I reply with another question, "What do you use today to stay in touch with leads and track current opportunities?" And since they expressed interest I name-drop a few of my competitors, "Do you use Salesforce.com or Sugar CRM and use ConstantContact or AWeber to send email blasts?"

The expert demonstrates his expertise by the questions he asks. This engages the prospect, and lets the prospect do the talking while giving you time to analyze their situation. Once you understand the strengths and weaknesses of their current state of affairs, you'll know how to position your goods and services.

Returning to my encounter above, the curious prospect might reply with, "Yes, we use Salesforce.com as our CRM and Constant Contact for email blasts—but we don't do that as often as we should—and my salespeople still rely on Outlook for day-to-day communications and once somebody buys, we basically lose track of them until they contact us with service work or to re-order, which most usually do eventually."

"Wow," I say. "What about new leads? How do you generate them? Are you getting them from your website or social media or at trade shows? How good are your salespeople at prospecting and networking and securing referrals and testimonials?"

Because I'm asking about key components of her sales and marketing plan that should already be in place, she assumes I am knowledgeable about those areas, which I am. And because I opened this conversation with the idea of automating all of these key components, I know her hot point. And because she keeps answering my questions, I know she is really interested in what I do, but I haven't told her exactly what I do, how long I've done it, whom I have helped or how much I charge.

She does not know my name, my company, my website. But I know I have a warm lead so I preempt her asking for my card—and I play hard to get—by replying, "I run across at least five people a day in your situation. I have to jump on a call right now, but if you're open to discussing this in more detail, I'd be happy to get your card and have my assistant reach out to set a time for us to speak later this week. Would that work for you?"

Non-Normal salespeople know the goal is not to see how many times they can give out their card. The goal is to see how many cards they can collect.

See the difference, my Abnormal Friend?
~☆~

Behold: The Weak Fold...Bold Grab Gold

Who are you?
What lights your fire?
What do you stand for?
What do your clients think you stand for?
What do you do better than anyone else in the world, or at least in your territory, state, city, zip code?
When was the last time you took a stand?
When was the last time you took a flying leap?
Has the economy sent you running with your tail between your legs or has it emboldened, empowered, emphasized and super-sized you?

The Bold Do Not Apologize For Who They Are

Do you want to be known? Do you want to gain "top-of-mind awareness" in the marketplace? Do you want to at least beat (if not totally bury, crush, send running for the hills) your competition? (If you're still reading, then you're my kind of motivated spirit!)

May I let you in on a little secret on how to accomplish the aforementioned?

- Take a stand.
- Choose to be excellent.
- Focus.
- Drive yourself.
- Stop making excuses.
- Raise your standards.
- Raise your expectations of those around you.
- Continue to learn.
- Take massive action.
- Eliminate negativity.
- Surround yourself with like-minded, action-oriented PRODUCERS!
- Never apologize for doing all of the above.

You Attract to the Same Degree You Repel

Barack Obama. Rush Limbaugh. Howard Stern. Sarah Palin. Just mentioning their names brings a smile or a scowl to your face. That's how they want it. They do it on purpose. They know that the motivated minority will beat the mediocre majority any day of the week and twice on Sunday.

These household names know their audiences and what motivates them. They take a stand and do what they have to do to motivate their supporters. They speak their minds. They are who they are. They're comfortable in their own skin. They know what they want and they go for it and they giggle and smirk and ignore the wishy-washy, couch-potato, afraid-to-draw-a-line-in-the-sand worriers that rely on better people to provide leadership, ingenuity and even security.

These leaders know that to those that oppose them they appear "fanatic and irrational." And they don't care. They didn't get their names in lights by watering down their beliefs and their messages for "broader appeal." FYI, you'll find many sell-outs, has-beens, one-hit-wonders, almost-presidents and hotel lobby cover bands that did. But that's not you, is it? You didn't start your business or get into sales to just be OK. But now times are tough and you're wondering, "What the heck did I get myself into?"

You're not alone.

But you know what? Nobody at the top got there alone, either. Obama, Limbaugh, Stern, Palin didn't get to where they are without a team including:

- Producers.
- Writers.
- Stylists.
- Marketing and Ad Agencies.
- Agents.
- Programmers.
- Web Designers.
- Assistants.
- Assistants to the Assistants.
- Chefs and Nutritionists.
- Personal Trainers.
- Pilots and chauffeurs and nannies and even guards.

You and me? We have each other. And as long as we have each other's back, that's enough.

Remember, Life is Good. It's "gooder" when you're bold. ~*~

The Blocking & Tackling Of Building A Business

Sell or Die

The fundamentals may not be fun but they win championships.

Today's economy (end of 2018) is pretty good but it will never be as good as it can be for those with their heads in the sand or other dark holes. If, however, you listen to my old linebacker coach at Air Force and "keep your head on a swivel" (translation: you're always looking around for threats and opportunities), you'll realize the great deals you can make as a business owner today.

Now's the time to get down to basics on your:

Overhead. Commercial properties are vacant. Renegotiate your rent. Maybe it's time to buy your own place. Find a bank that cares about you and understands your business. Haggle over your credit cards, hosting, vehicle lease, tech support and more. I bet with a little creativity and sticking to your guns you can add $500 to $5,000 a month to your bottom line just for asking...firmly.

Staff. Good people can be picked up for a fraction of what they would have cost you 24-36 months ago. Always be recruiting. Pay your staff for referrals that you hire. When you find a superstar, make room.

Advertising. Consumers are harder to reach than ever, but media buys are cheaper than ever for a few reasons: your competition is weak and cutting their marketing budgets; ad sales people forgot their fundamentals and are willing to cut deals because sales are down; and, online advertising is cutting into "traditional" media, which makes print and direct mail more affordable. Now's the time to increase your advertising and marketing budgets.

Technology. If you're doing something 2-3 times a day or even 4-5 times a week, you need to figure out how to automate it, especially your lead generation and follow-up sequences. Consumers are still buying. They're just more discerning with how they spend their hard-earned dollars. You need to be thorough, diligent and consistent with your sales process to win over these pickier prospects. Adopt the philosophy of "No lead left behind!"

Finances. 30-year rates are at all-time lows. I refinanced my home at 4.25% with no fees, no closing costs, no nothing other than an updated credit file and $20. This saves me almost $200/mo for the next 29 years and it took my wife and me maybe an hour to get everything together. Get your own financial house in order now. Get out of debt. Pay off high interest money with low interest money or just give it back. It's better to have cash and bad credit than no cash and bad credit.

Attitude. Most of us over-estimate what we can do in one year and under-estimate what we can do in five. Where's your head? In the clouds? In the sand? In a fog? Having goals and executing detailed plans diligently is important, but it's also hard to do. So surround yourself with people that can keep you on track and push you and pick you up and kick you in the rear when you need it.

Action. Knowledge is worthless. The massive application of knowledge is priceless. Many of your competitors are flubbing around like they've been zapped with a stun gun. While they fumble and mumble, you need to be moving forward rapidly with the support and advice of people that want to see you succeed. That's how the great quarterbacks and running backs live long enough in the NFL to reach the Hall of Fame.

Have you surrounded yourself with enough of those tough, supportive, team-oriented kinds of people? ~✶~

Life Is Worth Living. So Live It.

I may ramble a bit here. You've been warned.

On Oct 22, 2011, my 5th baby, (third girl) turned seven. Her name is Mary-Claire. (That's her turning three in the San Diego Children's Hospital below.*)

Having seven children with the same wife and no multiple births, we regularly hear creative, wise, loving people ask kind, sweet, thoughtful questions like:

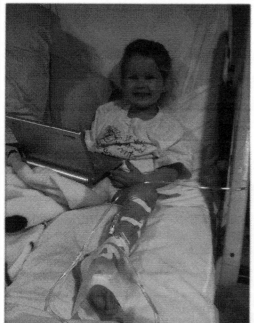

- *Are you done yet?* (Like a loaf of bread?)
- *Don't you know what causes that?* (Yes I do and I like it very much.)
- *Don't you own a TV?* (Do you have a nice one you want to get rid of?)
- *What, are you religious or something?* (Aren't you?)

- *When are you going to get fixed?* (EVERYTHING on me works just fine. Obviously.)

What's my point? I have a couple, maybe even a few.

1. Children are gifts from God. God does exist. God entrusts the miracle of life to us for a reason. That reason is not always readily apparent. Trust in God.

2. Life is fragile. Enjoy it. Appreciate it. Live it out loud and on purpose.
3. Fear keeps you from following your dreams.
4. 95% of fears never come true. 4% of our fears do come true, but aren't as bad as we feared. So 1% of potentially bad stuff is keeping you frozen, paranoid, stressed out, unhappy, grumpy, unproductive, limited, sad.
5. God did not work with your parents to bring you into this world to be poor and sad.

Go live on purpose. ~☆~

*Mary-Claire had an un-diagnosed ruptured appendix that took 15 days to identify and remove. (If this had happened just 100 years earlier she would have probably died.) I spent 11 days in the hospital with her. Her mommy spent all 15 days with her despite being 38 weeks pregnant with our fourth baby girl, Ella. Moms are the best, and Shannon's the best mommy. That's why we have seven kids, plus three miscarriages, which means we have three little angels pulling for us, praying for us, waiting for us in heaven and reminding God that we aren't "done like a loaf of bread," which is probably why Schaeffer Baby #7 came in April 2014, and is asleep on her big sister below as we dropped her off at her first day of college on 8/29/18. (And there's Mary-Claire, now nearly 14, smirking at her daddy taking more pictures.)

I told you life is a gift. Are you living each day like it is? ~☆~

What's Old Is New

Flap Your Gums &
Wag Your Tongue
To Sell More. Much More.

A few suggestions on how to succeed at selling today. Get...

* "Eyeball to eyeball."
* "Belly button to belly button."
* "Kneecap to kneecap."
* "Press the flesh."
* "Across the kitchen table."
* "Meet and greet."

Notice what is missing:

* "Twooting."
* "Facetubing."
* "Youbooking."
* "Blagging."
* "Social Messing."

My oldest, Jake, and me at a fort in India, March 2018

- "Text Interrupting."

Why don't more business owners and sales people work on their direct sales skills including prospecting, cold calling, mastering face-to-face interactions and their persuasion skills? A few reasons include...

Fear. Laziness. Wishful thinking. Shiny object chasing. Ignorance.

Marketing is just selling in print and most people are neither social or media masters. So if you can't sell the good ol' fashioned way, i.e., in person, you're gonna have a helluva time selling online, or in print, and 140 characters 10 times a day won't help you make your numbers.

You need to constantly improve your tongue-waggin' and gum-flappin' ability both over the phone and in person to get prospects and clients to make important decisions in a timely manner. Decisions such as:

- To confirm an appointment to meet with you,
- To evaluate your product,
- To introduce you to other decision-makers,
- To give you a deposit,
- To cut a PO,
- To take delivery of your product early,
- To provide a testimonial, a referral and/or a repeat order.

Why are you so afraid or hesitant? Maybe you're just comfortable or perhaps overwhelmed.

Regardless of the adjective that best describes you today, you will be living below your potential, which will make you grumpy, which will keep you even further under your potential, until you commit to your intended life's path and take massive action to head right on down that path today.

The good news is you don't have to come up for a new excuse for not growing, if that's the path you wish to take because excuses last forever. If you want this year to be better than last year bring in some new skills, which means bring in some old skills that everyone has forgotten or marginalized, which means they'll work again for you. ~*~

The Joy of Sales Leaders vs. Sales Managers

Make it happen or "staff" happens.

At the tender age of 29 I was promoted to general manager of an Oakwood Homes retail center in the thriving metropolis of Corinth, MS, population 11,002. Salute! (Any "Hee Haw" fans out there?)

I was a motivated, dedicated, caffeinated, decorated seller of mobile homes—manufactured homes, house trailers, tornado magnets—who had risen up quickly and stepped up to the plate when my District Manager was in need of assistance in cleaning up an under-performing store.

But I was concerned.

I knew I would have problems dealing with sales people that were not as fired up as me, sales people that weren't willing to show up early, stay late, do the right thing and get the job done no matter what it took.

And I was right. And it was hard.

When I arrived, I inherited 4 human beings whose employee files said "Sales." But you can't believe everything you read, so I quickly went to work figuring out who was a "keeper," who was a "fixer-upper," and who was a "let-em-goer" while simultaneously placing ads to recruit more talent into that little store to help me reach the aggressive sales goals my district manager set.

The concept of "Hire Slow. Fire Fast." served me well during that venture.

There was some wailing and gnashing of teeth those first few weeks but after 30 days everyone knew I was there to lead, not to manage. They also knew I could sell, and that I would sell regardless the circumstances.

I didn't seek friends. I sought sales. And I rewarded those that "got it" and "got with it" by stepping up their own efforts.

Too many sales "managers" spend too much time on the dogs and ignore the eagles. To lead a sales team, focus on those that seek growth, ideas, guidance and leadership.

Sidebar: By "ignore," I mean don't waste time, money, effort or thought on the under-performers. Just put them on notice that they have 30-90 days to improve their sales dramatically or they are gone, while you simultaneously EXPAND your recruiting efforts to replace the turnover all sales organizations experience. Those that have pride and desire to excel in sales will seek your counsel. You can help them. Cut the rest. Need to get better at this? Check out **NoMoreSalesDuds.com**.

Did my approach work?

The store was losing $63,000/mo when I arrived. In 90 days, we turned a $1,000 profit with only two of the first four original sales people on the staff.

14 years later, I'm still friends with those two sales people because I led and worked with those that wanted to perform to my standards. I'm also still friends with the store manager that gave me my start and recommended me for the promotion because we are kindred spirits.

Are you ready to build businesses and friendships that last and make more money along the way?

Raise your level of expectations of your staff, your vendors and everyone with whom you work.
Lead by example.
See disasters like losing $63,000 per month as an opportunity to shine.

Hire slow, fire fast.
Always be recruiting.
Learn how to sell.
Keep reading this book. ~✶~

Does Your "Why" Make You Cry?

Are your soul and heart, mind and attention, blood, tears and sweat given to that which occupies your *workaday* life? Does a tear (or three) literally wet your eyes when you fall short of your daily, weekly or annual goals?

Or do you find yourself going through the motions? Doing the minimum to make the boss happy or to keep clients from complaining?

Until you are so passionate about your "why" you actually cry when you don't reach your goals, you will find your career (and probably your life) a few fries short of a Happy Meal.

Last year your goals were either:

- Met.
- Exceeded.
- Far exceeded.
- Missed.
- Absent.

- Wrong.

Beautiful. That's why you must always take a few moments—even days—to evaluate the past and prepare for the future on a regular basis, which means more than once every five years.

In today's new economy (how many "new" economies can we really have?) of global competition, back-stabbing politicians, defaulting governments, and confusing numbers as it pertains to the actual levels of unemployment and under-employment, you REALLY need to do this.

Now more than ever, you must question EVERYTHING including:

- What is "The American Dream" and is it your dream or Madison Avenue's dream or Freddie Mac's dream?
- Is a corporation-under-funded pension or a gyrating 401(k) really the foundation of your "golden years?"
- Do you really have to wait until you're 65 or 75 to have "golden years?"
- Are one or two or 435 corrupt politicians with their hands in the pockets of lobbyists the only way jobs (your job?) will be created next year?
- Why does that schmuck down the street make more money, drive a nicer car, and smile more than you when you know more than he does, work harder than he does, are more likable than he is and care more about your clients than he ever will?

Now's the time to bust out your history books—the REAL history books—and internalize what it took to discover and colonize this nation, to fight against the most powerful nation in the world for our freedom, to head West (with no pension or unemployment or government health care) as part of our Manifest Destiny, and to become the most powerful nation in our own right.

You have it in you to create your own Manifest Destiny. You have it in you to forge your own path to success as defined by you.

Yeah, yeah, I know. The economy is tough.

You know what? It won't get better any time soon, which begs the question: How long will you use the excuse of the economy (or some other convenient, publicly-acceptable "reason") to put off your own goals, dreams and desires?

No one we know of ever did anything worth a damn by "waiting it out," "hunkering down," or "keeping their heads down."

2011-2018 were great years for me.

I invested in more training programs, more certifications, more partnerships, more affiliate relationships, more group and private coaching, and read more books on sales, marketing and persuasion than any year in my life.
The results?

I have a home office I love. My staff is lean, mean, and 100% virtual. I wrote my first book in 2012 and I wrote the first edition of this second book in 2013, with the updated and re-branded edition released in late 2018. I have another two books already in the works for next year. I travel only when I want to so I'm home for volleyball, soccer, meeting boyfriends, helping with homework, and taking my wife to dinner. I make all of their school events, exercise 5-7 days a week, and have total control over my schedule and my life.

Is it any surprise to learn that I'm closing bigger deals, being asked to speak on more stages, and have more varied streams of income than ever before? On purpose. By design.

Why? Because my why makes me cry. Does yours? ~✳~

"Novelisters" & Marketers: How To Make Small Things Interesting

Arthur Schopenhauer was a smart German dude who did a lot of

pondering and writing. (He sure didn't spend much time on his hair...or did he?) His ideas influenced the thinking of some other smart dudes like Einstein, Jung and Freud.

Today, 155+ years after his death, he is still influencing thinkers, business owners, marketers and sales people alike, especially with his quote "The business of the novelist is not to relate great events, but to make small ones interesting."

You are probably not a novelist. Neither am I. We are, however, engaged in commerce and commerce needs sales people to survive and sales people need good marketing to keep from working themselves to death.

When you study great marketing, you see how they make the small details interesting. Don Draper in "Mad Men" came up with the idea to stress the "obvious" fact that Lucky Strike tobacco is toasted...just like their competitors. They were just the first to make a big deal out of it.

Coors Light is "frost brewed." That's a "secret recipe," right? Actually, they are just following John Palmer's advice who wrote the book "How to Brew", a guide to home brewing. Brewing beer at 34 degrees is precisely the temperature he suggests for making *cerveza* in your kitchen.

Making small details interesting made these brands household names.

What small detail about your services and offerings do you take for granted, over-look and under-exploit to your own detriment? We all suffer from being too close to our business. We get comfortable—and bored—and we make the deadly assumption that our prospects either know or do not care to know about the little diamonds in our roughness.

Are you skipping over your own toasted, your own frost-brewing, your own diamond? Are you sure? Despite Rebecca's experience and expertise she was open to my assistance. Here are the results… ~✭~

> "I have had the pleasure of working with Wes Schaeffer for four years in my role with Infusionsoft, and Wes has continually impressed me. As a partner he has done a fantastic job consulting with clients and helping them achieve success with Infusionsoft.
>
> "And recently we have engaged with him to write copy and I was really excited to get Wes' copy back because it was personal; it was targeted; it was funny—it was really funny, which is difficult to do in writing
>
> "Not only did he write fantastic copy, he gave us two options to test and choose the one gave that us the best possible results. Quick turnaround, easy person to work with, and all around a really great person who knows what he's about.
>
> "In his copywriting services or in general Infusionsoft consulting, Wes Schaeffer is your guy."
>
> **Rebecca Sprynczynatyk**
> **Products Marketing Manager**
> **Infusionsoft**

Deliver a Powerful Message In a Powerful Manner

"Extra! Extra! Read All About It!"

"That's the way it is," comforted Walter Cronkite every evening.

Ahhhh. The good ol' days.

- ABC, CBS, NBC and those fuzzy UHF channels. (Remember that dial below the main dial with all the numbers on them?)
- Stations actually shut down or "signed off" at midnight by playing the National Anthem and you had to wait until 6 am to watch anything again.
- AM radio was for farm reports and country music.
- Talk radio was for preachers.
- Al Gore hadn't invented the internet.
- Spiegel sent 6 pound catalogs.
- The postman knew your name and actually brought letters, written by hand, to your door.

Then WHAM! Welcome to the good new technology days!! (Can you believe yesterday and today are the "good ol' days" for our kids?)

- "You may already be a winner!"

- "I am Mr. Emory Barr, Accounts Manager, of Abbey National PLC Bromley Rd Branch. I have an important business proposition for you."
- "Text the word VOTE to win!"
- "But wait! Operators are standing by! If you're one of the first 77 callers we'll QUADRUPLE your order!"

We now receive more interruptions and offers and advertisements per hour than we got per week just 10 years ago. Today's ads are more targeted, focused, *"interrupt-ative"* and pervasive than anything the "Madmen" on Madison Avenue could have ever postulated over their two-martini, three-hour lunches 55 years ago. (But those are the books we read and that's what marketing degrees are build on. How's that working out for you?)

Thanks to technology, we are both better and less-informed depending on whether we are burying our heads in video games to escape reality or reading the news to appreciate the escapes our video games bring.

How are we, as business owners, to penetrate this electronic shield to reach our ideal prospects and convince them that we are their only choice?

5 Words: Consistency. Frequency. Breadth. Relevance. Transparency.

Easy to say. Hard to do.

If you're like most people with products to sell and businesses to grow, you're probably a sales "dabbler." By that I mean you're not really sure what works when it comes to advertising and marketing so you dabble in radio then TV then the Yellow Pages then direct mail then email blasts and while you're on blasts let's throw in text messaging and voicemail broadcasts then mail a newsletter a couple of times until you realize how hard and expensive that is so you plan a couple of webinars, which make newsletters seem like a cake walk so you hire someone to help you with Google AdWords until you've depleted your beer and pizza cash for the quarter with no increase in leads so you turn to blogging and social media since everyone is online and besides, it's free, right?

Told ya. You're a dabbler.
"Fine, Wes. You got me. I'm a dabbler. Where should I market my business?" Everywhere you can.

"What medium should I use?" Whichever one gives you the best ROI.

"How many different marketing mediums should I use?" As many as you can and still have a positive ROI.

"What should I say?" **FINALLY,** you're asking the right question!

Despite what the 140-character micro-bloggers of the world would like you to believe, CONTENT IS STILL KING and will be FOREVER! If you can deliver a powerful message in a powerful manner, it will find the right person that will invest in what you have to offer.

"But, Wes, I'm not a writer!" Does your why make you cry? Do you know your business better than anyone else? Do you provide a better product or service than your competition? Do you feel the pain of your clients?

Tell THAT story in an authentic manner and let me know how that works for you. I'll bet a dollar to a doughnut you'll be pleased with the results.

"But, Wes, Where do I tell it?" Start with your webcam on your computer or your smartphone camera and just speak your mind and upload it to YouTube and embed it on your social media sites and ask your friends to give you feedback. Then have it transcribed and embed that along with the video on your blog or website and Tweet it out to the world and send an email to your client and prospect list and say "Hey, what do you think of me using technology?"

They'll think you're Walter Cronkite. And that is the way it is. ~*~

Sleeping Prospects Do Not Buy!

How To Be More Interesting In Your Prospecting and Selling Endeavors

Ever heard the story of having the faith of a 1mm diameter Brassica juncea?

Me neither.

But we've all heard the parable of Jesus telling us to have faith the size of a mustard seed.

Why a mustard seed? Because it's one of the smallest seeds on the planet. Jesus was making a point and he used stories and examples that people of his time could relate to in order to do so.

Facts tell. Stories sell.

You want to sell more, right?

Why aren't you telling more stories?

"Wes, what kind of story can I tell about wedding planning, trash collection, IT services or cosmetic surgery?"

Oh ye with the creativity of a mustard seed!

I worked with a client who sold commercial trash services. (Who knew that businesses have a choice when it comes to who picks up their trash? Apparently the big guys don't want you to know you do have a choice.)

So as I asked him what makes his company special he said they are locally owned and operated, certified and insured, yada, yada, yada...and take the time to deodorize the big trash bins at a client's office each week, to which I replied,

"Holy cow! How nice is that! I've been by some DISGUSTING trash bins at offices, restaurants, stadiums and it reflects poorly on them and makes me not want to return. You need to play that up!"

"Really?" he said.

I told him the story of the plumbing company that focused on the fact that their plumbers didn't stink. (Mike Diamond here in SoCal.)

We both chuckled at that but he got the point. He's now writing a free report as a Lead Magnet and one of the questions he'll answer is "Do my dumpsters have to stink?"

Now is any property manager or comptroller of a building really asking that question on a regular basis? Probably not.

Have they all asked that question at least once or twice during their business careers? Yes.

Will they ask it now? You bet.

In Lori Silverman's book "Wake Me Up When The Data Is Over", she reminds us, "Facts inform, stories resonate. Facts are filed away. Stories inspire and connect to deeper currents that move us to reflection and inspiration."

Lori tells stories about Microsoft, Verizon and even my good ol' U.S. Air Force, who are now telling stories to make a point, motivate employees and win new customers.

The late, great Zig Ziglar told stories and that worked out okay for him. Jesus told stories and we're still reading and retelling them 2,118 years later.

Now stories about stinky dumpsters are being told in Florida, and I bet the "big guys" are smelling defeat.

What's your story? ~✶~

Celebrating the Spirited Entrepreneur

Courage. Guts. Bravery.

I have a confession to make. I woke up at 2:30 AM today.
I wish I could say it was an isolated event but, suffice it to say, the roosters are moving away because I've put them out of work.

Entrepreneurs realize every day we must run, fast. Sometimes we're the lion, sometimes the gazelle. But sitting still is not an option. You (we), the Entrepreneur, the Business Owner, the Sales Professional who only gets paid when a sale is made, delivered, and a satisfied client remits payment, cannot sit still.

Why?

* It's not in your DNA.
* You know there are great perils present today.
* You know there are great opportunities present today.
* You know security can only be found in two places:
* Federal prisons.
* Bringing value to your clients.

You bring value to your clients by staying current on industry trends and the needs of your clients and conveying to them on a consistent basis that you are ready, willing and capable of helping them address their needs, wants, desires and fears.

Performing Without a Net Takes G.U.T.T.S.S.

Monuments aren't erected in honor of the middle-manager with the fewest paper cut-related incidents in a calendar month. Trophies aren't named after the sales person who mailed out the most company brochures to prospects who were blowing him off. Scholarships aren't created to celebrate the business owner with the most forgettable ad.

Nope.
To make it—to really stand out—to KICK ASS AND TAKE NAMES, requires you to:

* Surround yourself with excellence.
* Take massive action.
* Offend. And Not apologize.
* Practice. Drill. Rehearse.
* Measure. Test.
* Delegate. Inspect.

- Wash. Rinse. Repeat.

But that takes...

- Effort. Energy.
- Focus. Accountability.
- Stamina. Creativity.
- New Ideas. New Processes.
- New Technology.
- Encouragement.
- Masterminds.
- G.U.T.S.S.

Where can you find all of that? You won't find it in the concentrated abundance you need at a networking group or a free seminar or for sale in "Sky Mall" magazine.

Nope. No way. No how.

You'll only find them via total immersion with like-motivated, same-minded, unapologetic achievers. You see, pros like to hang around pros. It's not lonely at the top. It's actually a lot more giving and open and friendlier at the top. There is less posturing, less posing, less drama and less bullshit. People of excellence do not have time to dilly-dally or dawdle.

And thriving necessitates excellence.
And necessity is the mother of invention.
And learning is the key to invention.
And repetition is the key to learning.

Now you have a choice:
- Put down this book and get back to the urgent, but not important.
- Mark this page for review and get back to the important, but not urgent.
- Ignore this message for three weeks only to find out you put off too long doing what needed to be done, which, not-coincidentally, is the root of many of your problems.

Turn to the **Resources** section in the back of this book right now and enroll now in the most innovative, comprehensive sales, marketing, thinking and attitude training you have ever had the opportunity to join.

The choice is yours. Choose wisely. ~✱~

P.S. G.U.T.S.S stands for Gain Unlimited Tools and Techniques for Sales Success. It's a comprehensive training program I am creating as this book goes to print, so stay tuned for more resources to help you grow your sales, such as **www.MakeEverySale.com**.

Hey, sidebar:

Do you know what takes guts? Seeking help to save your marriage after you wanted to end your marriage, reversing your vasectomy, then quitting your successful jobs in Corporate America to make your misery your ministry.

That's what my friends Greg and Julie Alexander did and they have been blessed and rewarded with a growing family, a growing non-profit, and a growing for-profit business.

Hear their story on episode 74 of The Sales Podcast, which you can access at **TheSalesWhisperer.com/session74**. Man does not live on bread alone. Let me know what you think of their story.

Now go listen to something!

Desiderius Erasmus

"In regione caecorum rex est luscus."
"In the land of the blind, the one-eyed man is king."
~ Desiderius Erasmus Roterodamus

"The lamp of the body is the eye." (Lamps shed light. Light dispels the dark. Monsters lurk in the dark. So light dispels monsters.)

"If your eye is sound," (Do you have fully charged batteries in your flashlight? If not, you merely have a large paper weight. You cannot be productive if you cannot focus and you cannot focus in the dark.)

"…your whole body will be filled with light;" (When your workplace is full of light, you are energized because you can focus. When you concentrate on the task at hand, it leaves no room for doubt or fear or darkness or boogie-men.)

"…but if your eye is bad, your whole body will be in darkness." ("Quiet on the set! Lights out! Cue scary music! Release the monsters! Run! Be afraid!")

"And if the light in you is darkness, how great will the darkness be." (Hello doubt, confusion, indecision, inaction, loss, despair, failure, unemployment, breadlines, government handouts, loss of the Pioneer Spirit, loss of guts.)
~ Jesus as quoted in Matthew Chapter 6
(The brackets are mine.)

Harvey Penick, the greatest golf instructor of all time, taught his students such as Tom Kite, Ben Crenshaw and Mickey Wright to "take dead aim."

If you are a golfer, you know that your bad shots, your disasters, your yanks, your chili-dips, your skulled smiley-faces, your bananas, your club-throwing, golf-god-cursing shots occur when you are focused on what could go wrong rather than on the target.

Napoleon Hill, who wrote the greatest personal-success book of all time, "Think and Grow Rich," taught us the power of the Master Mind.

And Stephen Covey, author of the greatest self-help book since I was born, "The Seven Habits of Highly Effective People" reminds us of the power of habits, both good and bad, and we all know it takes at least 21 days to form or break a habit. (It could take longer or shorter depending on the root emotion, the neuropeptide connection the behavior has, and your motivation, which brings into play things such as attitude, adrenaline levels, experiences, expectations and more. But everyone knows the 21-day concept so let's continue, shall we?)

If I was a gambling man, I'd say it has been more than 21 days since...

You re-charged your own batteries.
The monsters started coming out from under your bed and made a home in your head.
Your focus became fragmented, distracted, blurred.
You participated in a Master Mind group whose members wanted nothing more than to find ways to help you succeed.
You began questioning your sanity as to why you were in business in the first place!

Am I right?

Choices:

Life is full of choices: coffee or tea? Donut or fruit? Gym or snooze? Pity party or celebration of excellence? Turn the page or take action?

One simple, affordable, interactive, protected way to take action is to enroll in one of many live and/or virtual training programs listed in the Resources section in the back of the book.

Need to get better at sales? **www.MakeEverySale.com**.

Need to hire better sales people? **NoMoreSalesDuds.com**.

Need to get better with your sales and marketing automation? Infusionsoft Mastermind (It's great even if you don't own Infusionsoft because we get into the thinking and the strategies behind the technology.)

Need one-on-one time with me? I have 90-day and 12-month options.

Need the entire team at The Sales Whisperer®? Contact Us.

Need something local? Start looking and if you can't find it, start a group of your own. The teacher ALWAYS learns more than the student.

When & If you do that, you'll experience what Erasmus meant because you'll see that everyone around you is running blind. Be their eyes—just one eye—and enjoy being King or Queen.

Remember, Life is good. It's "gooder" when you see clearly. ~*~

3 Frogs, New Year Resolutions, And a Gift

A New Year's Day Quiz to cut through the New Year's Eve celebratory fog:

Three frogs are sitting on a stump. One decided to jump off. How many are left? If you're an analytical type you say, "Like, duh, 3 minus 1 = 2." If you're a Southerner like me you say, "Well dang. Anybody that's ever seen frogs in da rivah (translation: "the river") knows that when one frog jumps off they all jump off. So the answer is zero!"

If you're wise beyond your years, you say, "The answer is three because the first frog has not yet jumped. It only made a decision to jump."

What did you decide to do last year that you did not actually do? To make that "not-getting-done" list shorter this year, decide this very second just one thing you want to achieve this year. Literally. Right now.

Stop reading this article and do it this exact moment in time.
Stop reading and write down what it is you are going to do this year.
Type it and print it, write it in a journal, write it on a sticky note, whatever.

But write it, put a date on it, make it visible and get started on it right now even if takes you 5 hours, 42 minutes and 17 seconds.
Football games are not that important. (Really. They aren't.)

Parades are not that important.

Putting away the dishes or your decorations are not that important.
Neither is chatting with Facebook friends, updating your Fantasy Football league, washing the cat or reading your horoscope ("You'll experience something wonderful today and someone important will come into your life or leave your life." Your horoscope is now up to date for the year.)

After you
1) decide,
2) document and
3) DO,…

Visit the link in the Resources section under the title of this article for your free gift. (Warning: It requires more effort but a millionaire told me he does this a couple of times a year so I'm giving you the clues to success that I've been given.)

This is the year of getting really important, meaningful, profitable, impactful things done.

Are you a decider or doer? ~✻~

"In 87 days we added 22 new students to our daycare, which has added $250,000 to our annual bottom line."
~Kevin & Becky Patrick

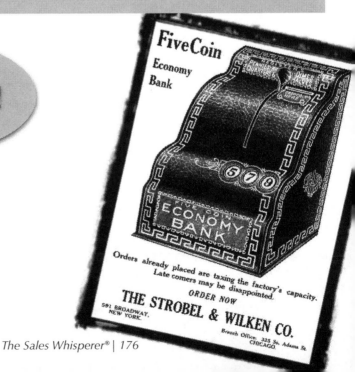

Hey, Baby, What's Your Number?

How To Set Your Sales Number For The Year

(We'll talk about how to MAKE that number next.)

Between Wednesday, November 24th, 2010 and Saturday, January 1st, 2011 I lost 10.5 pounds. No, I was not sick, thank you very little. I lost the weight on purpose.

How? Five key factors contributed to my success:

1. I knew my starting point. (That's easy for all of us, although few of us want to admit how deep of a rut we may be in at the moment...so face your fears to conquer them.)
2. I knew my TRUE goal. (Not as easy. I have struggled my entire life to set and work towards specific, true goals and I am convinced we are more afraid of success than failure. Put something down on paper now and start moving towards it.)
3. I knew the date of my goal. (A goal without a date is just a dream.)
4. I knew EXACTLY what I had to do EVERY DAY to reach my goal. (Here's where I make my money day in and day out. Making the rubber hit the road. Details and accountability. Most of us have big "dreams" but don't know what to do for the next 37 minutes to begin getting there. THIS can get you over that hurdle.)
5. I was motivated to get there because I had a physique that was less than stellar for the first time in my life. (No one can give you desire.)

To grow your income, you need to increase your sales. To increase your sales, you need to know your numbers. The key numbers you need to know are your:

- **Target revenue.** If your average sale is $1,000 and you want to gross $10,000 per month, you need to close 10 deals per month.
- **Closing ratio.** If 50% of the people that request a proposal place an order, you need to make 20 proposals a month.
- **Proposal ratio.** If 50% of the people that you meet with ask for a proposal, you need to have 40 meetings a month.
- **Appointment ratio.** If 20% of the people you speak with agree to meet, you need to speak with 200 people a month.
- **Conversation ratio.** If 20% of

your calls to reach a decision maker result in a conversation, you need to make 1,000 dials a month.

- **Prospecting efficiency.** 1,000 dials a month equals nearly 48 dials a day assuming 21 business days in a month. You should be able to make 48 dials of the phone in 2—2.5 hours, which leaves plenty of time to update your Facebook, talk some smack in your Fantasy Football League, make your daily presentations and close deals.

Would you like to make fewer calls and make more money?

- Raise your prices and/or
- Get better at closing, and/or
- Make better appointments, and/or
- Get better on the phone by,
- Learning to engage and connect with receptionists and executive assistants, and/or
- Get the attention of decision makers on the phone, and/or
- Get a better list of prospects to talk to.

I haven't had to make outbound prospecting calls since 2007. But I made a crapload of them for a decade: literally, from 1997 to 2007. I got good on the phone and face-to-face, which laid the foundation for me to become a great marketer.

But I still have to sell. My marketing "warms up" or "softens" my prospects, but most still want to speak with me, to connect, to question, to have their final concerns addressed.

My numbers today are different but the same. I'm tracking website visitors, page views, time on site and bounce rates. I'm tracking opt-ins, repeat visitors, requests for demonstrations and discussions. And I'm still tracking proposals, Win/Loss ratios, testimonials, referrals and upsells.

It all goes back to "you can't expect what you don't inspect." As a motivated entrepreneur you get bored, anxious and turned off looking at spreadsheets and reports but they are vital to the growth of your business. To get to the upper-echelon of your industry, you must know where you are, where you're coming from and where you're going.

Remember Erasmus a few pages back? With just one eye you can be King. Since it's easier to open both eyes at the same time, start there.

The world is ready for you to see it and to prosper from it. Are you ready to see what it has in store for you? ~☆~

Half A Mile From Shore Without A Boat

That's the actual island I swam to in June 2012. Anthony Vela took the photo of Maggie Adams who runs SupTrotters.com.

Achieving goals is in the human DNA.

Half a mile is just two laps around a 400 meter track. You could walk it in about 5 minutes. You could drive it in about 30 seconds, with your satellite radio, GPS and A/C on, Starbucks in one hand, iPhone in the other, and you can stop at any time.

When you swim half a mile out in the open ocean it takes more than a minute or even 10…and you have to swim back…and you can stop at any time...if you want to die.

In June 2012 I took a little family trip to San Clemente, CA. Some friends from Texas were visiting and we hung out on the beach and celebrated my wife's birthday on the 20th while the kids smushed pennies on the Amtrak Surfliner rails.

We had never been to this beach, and as soon as my buddy John and I stepped foot on the sand, we saw some rocks off in the distance. Like macho men with egos much larger than our brains, we said *"Let's swim out to those rocks."* Our wives both looked at each other and said, *"Why does that not surprise us?"*

The "problem" is I was only half serious. I'm happy sitting under an umbrella reading all week while John needs to compete every waking moment (and every other sleeping moment). He was raring to go.

So we goof off a couple of days, go to San Diego for Shannon's birthday, and then THE time arrived. The swim time. John says, *"You ready?"* I say, *"Yes"* (but not meaning it). Off we go.

If you've never swum (swim, swam, swum, right?) long distances and/or in the open ocean, I would recommend against just *doing it.* I'm a fine swimmer but I had never trained for open-water swimming at that point, had never gone that far in the open ocean, but I knew I could do it. I just didn't NEED to do it.

As we were swimming along, we'd pause for a moment to catch our breath and I'd tell John, *"I'm happy to go back any time you are."* But we were always *"Almost there."* So we continued.

Crazy thoughts go through your mind as you are bobbing on the waves seven football fields from shore:

- What is under me?
- Will I get tangled in the kelp and drown? (Why didn't I bring a knife?)
- I'm swimming to a rock piled high with seals. Sharks eat seals.
- How will I get on that rock with the waves and barnacles and jagged edges?
- Will I get there only to get attacked by a big seal? (Do seals kill people? Why didn't I bring a knife? Are seals protected? Would my kids prefer me to stab a seal and live or know I was peaceful and loving as I let a big seal maul me to death?)
- Will I get a cramp and drown?
- If a shark bites me, which limb would I prefer to lose or would I just want to die? (Why didn't I bring a knife?)
- Sure, we told the lifeguards we were going out but they can't reach us if we get into trouble.
- Is that a riptide I'm swimming against?
- Am I going to get within 100 yards of shore and get driven head first into the sand by the breaking waves I can't handle because I'm too tired coming back to shore?

Those thoughts were all natural (unfortunately) but they were all fleeting (by design). I say "by design" because I did receive some excellent training at the Air Force Academy on remaining calm during stressful situations. As a salesman and sales trainer, I've also received some excellent training on the power of positive thinking and setting goals. Finally, those thoughts were fleeting because I had a good partner. I didn't jump into that ocean alone. John and I stuck together and created a great memory by achieving a goal we set together, albeit quickly and with more than a smidgen of bravado.

When we returned to land, our wives jokingly ran up to us like we were long lost sailors and hugged us and told us they could see us standing on the rock and they thought it was pretty cool. (And they were glad they weren't going to have to raise 11 kids between them without their husbands!)

What are your goals?

- Start your own company?
- Sell more in your current job?
- Run a marathon?
- Lose weight?
- Write a book?
- Learn a new language?
- All of the above?

What are you doing about it?

- Playing Farmville or Candy Crush on Facebook?
- Griping about the lack of support from your employer?
- Whining about how tough the economy is?
- Filling your mind with good, positive, educational stuff such as free podcasts—**TheSalesPodcast.com**—reading books on sales (thanks for reading this book and reading this far) and goal setting and finding a sales mentor and/or mastermind group to help you get where you want and NEED to go now?!

The big rock is waiting for you. You can reach it. Thinking about it won't help. Deciding to do it won't get you to it. Taking action and moving towards it will.

Achieving and abundance and prosperity is what you were made for.

Get a partner and dive in. ~✰~

Who's Pushing You?

(Kids Provide The Best Sales Coaching)

"Ella Bella" is 4 in this picture.
She's riding a bike without training wheels for the first time.
Ella smiled.
Decker, the dog, barked.
Olivia, the neighbor, cheered.
Shannon, the mom pondered, "All six of our kids can now swim and ride a bike. They're growing up so fast." (Two years later she's pregnant with #7. Careful what you wish for.)

Are you still growing up or do you find yourself unwilling or unable to take the training wheels off your:

- Business?
- Relationships?
- Health?
- Fitness?
- Finances?
- Faith?

To ride her bike all by herself, Ella first had to see her friend and fellow-4-year old ride her bike with no training wheels. (Someone set the example.) Then her mom and I removed the training wheels and supported her while she mastered the new skill. (Someone guided her along the way.)

Finally, her friends and family gathered 'round to cheer her on and console her when she fell and to encourage her to get back on. (Someone motivated her to continue.)

Where do you get your motivation, your inspiration, your support? Who sets the example for you to follow? When you have six kids, you live in a sales coaching lab because kids are born salesmen. They fight and persuade and sell their way with their siblings and their parents every day. They need no sales coaching.

To reach your goals, you can "invest" in more kids and observe their sales tenacity "patiently" for the next 10 years, or you can keep going it alone, or your can invest in professional, private sales coaching and masterminds.

My Pre-Paid Sales Advisor—www.PrePayWes.us—program is reassuringly expensive, which is why you'll focus, listen and apply what you learn during our time together. Which is why you'll grow.

Are the products and services you offer "reassuringly expensive?" Would you like them to be?

Do you need a little push to get there? ~*~

Masterpieces Aren't Made In A Clean Kitchen

My dad is *(in)famous* for saying, "When you're waist-deep in alligators, it's hard to remember that your goal was to drain the swamp."

Growing up in Louisiana, that was a relevant analogy because swamps—and alligators—are everywhere down there.

If your'e not from from the South, your dad may have said, "Masterpieces aren't made in a clean kitchen."

I tell you this because the business of business is messy. But you know what? So is life. So is being an employee. So is being in love, being married, being a parent, being alive and interacting with fellow humans. But it's worth living and it's worth living well.

You're in sales and/or in business to provide a good or a service that solves problems for your clients. In the world of sales, though, we, our clients, and our marketplace face new problems daily. These new problems must be solved if you are to be paid and because you can solve them better than anyone else you A) are in business and B) get paid better than anyone else for doing so. If you do not have the ability to apply the attention, the focus and the solutions required by the marketplace to solve problems, the end is near, whether you know it or not.

But, keeping your finger on the pulse of what the marketplace wants, needs and demands takes effort. Designing, re-designing, launching, re-launching, negotiating, purchasing, testing, marketing and selling, partnering, sourcing raw materials, new suppliers and vendors and resellers, building prototypes, conducting surveys and polls and turning a profit takes effort.

Meanwhile, your customer is banging his fork on the table screaming, "I'M HUNGRY AND IF YOU DON'T BRING ME WHAT I WANT RIGHT NOW I'M LEAVING AND GOING ACROSS THE STREET AND I'M GOING ON TWITTER AND FACEBOOK AND YELP AND TELLING THE WORLD HOW SLOW YOUR SERVICE IS! BRING ME MY FOOD!"

When the yelling from the client reaches a crescendo a week, a month, or a quarter before your masterpiece is out of the oven, the thought will cross your mind to just throw in the towel, lock the doors, turn off the lights and post your resume to Monster.com.

But as you are walking through your messy kitchen of a business, you are distracted by a ringing phone. Your best waitress calls in sick. As you hang up, you get another call and two of your busboys are hungover. Your phone rings again, and it's your top chef calling to inform you he wants a raise or he's leaving to open a competitive restaurant next door. Then your software vendor calls to tell you there is a bug in the Point of Sale system and you'll have to reboot all of your machines, which will take at least an hour before they are all back online.

In a bewildered, mesmerized fog you robotically, habitually answer the phone one last time and the biggest food critic in town is on the other end of the line calling to tell you that after 6 months of invitations, she's coming in to your "messy kitchen" tonight, with a film crew, "to see what all the buzz is about."

Finally. Your big break.
The moment you've been waiting for.
You're so thrilled you don't even get upset when a guest tells you the toilet is overflowing because his kid threw his Tonka® truck in it.

Nope. You do what any good entrepreneur would do: you solve the issues by taking quick, decisive action. You prioritize. You focus. You delegate. You win by being in the moment when your opportunity presented itself...

...but you aren't gonna lie. You're tired...

...and you question your sanity for ever wanting to drain the swamp, or make the masterpiece...

You may become frustrated that despite your best efforts and intentions to plan and prioritize and "catch up" (can someone define that for me?) you're still behind. Your desk is a mess. Your car is a mess. Your hair is too long. Your temper is too short. Your Starbuck's barista knows you by name. Your fitness trainer has forgotten your name. Your dog thinks your neighbors are his owner. Your car windshield has "wash me" chiseled in the dust. Your meals are eaten at your desk (when you have time to eat) and you haven't said hello to your mom in two weeks...

...but you are winning...

...because you are not quitting.

You're learning where the saying "tough times don't last, tough people do" came from and you are questioning whether or not you are tough enough. Let me tell your something. Not only are you tough, you are the Navy SEAL of American enterprise. You are the toughest. You are the strongest. You are the most capable because you passed on the opportunity of a "safety net" Corporate America says they provide and you have entered the arena of the entrepreneur, the professional sales person, the business owner.

Your competition is fading and they do not have the resolve you do. Surround yourself with like-minded, driven, hard-headed, determined entrepreneurs that can encourage you to stay the course and complete the mission.

It will not always be this tough if you stay true to yourself and your dreams and your goals. The grass is not greener "over there" and it still needs mowing. The alligators will go away. The flour and the sauce will be wiped off the counter later tonight.

Enjoy the fact that you are doing what no one else can because, soon, no one else will.

When that moment arrives—and trust me, it will come—when you can breathe again, you will breathe the clean, the pure, the un-crowded, rarified air that can only be found at the top, and you will gulp it in, then sip it in, then soak in it with no guilt, no shame—only pride—and you will know you are worthy of partaking that air and you will know the struggle was worth it.

I'm proud of you. ~☀~

Hey, sidebar:

Why are you so afraid of doing something new? Is it because you're afraid to fail or because your'e afraid that others will see where you're starting from and think "Wow. I thought she was farther along/more successful than that"?

Dive in. Be bold. Move fast. Break things. There is so little you know or can know until you launch.

So as Roy H. Williams would say, "Pull the trigger and ride the bullet."

And if you need some help making your CRM, shopping cart, or email marketing platform hum, check out **TheCRMButler.com**.

Waist-deep In Alligators

I have a few confessions and statements-of-the-obvious to make:

- life is hard.
- building a business is hard.
- being a good husband is hard.
- being a good parent is hard.
- living your faith is hard.
- getting that last piece of ice off the bottom of the plastic cup is REALLY hard.

But they are all worth doing. In fact, anything worth doing is worth doing poorly until you master it. Like you, over the past several years, I've been working on doing all of the above and I have experienced varying degrees of success and failure. Over this time I have learned some sobering facts:

- most of the "got-it-together" people you see do not have it together...at all!
- most are faking it until they maybe make it.
- most of the gurus do not live their own advice.
- most of the experts are either wrong or just in it for the money.

Where does that leave you and me?

Enjoy the journey.
Take pride in the little victories.
Test the advice of the "gurus" but save your worship for the Lord.
Bite off more than you can chew.
Outsource what you're no good at.
Create business systems so you can be free.
Read more joke books.

Why am I telling you this? I don't know.

Part of it is because I'm tired and I feel bad that I haven't written in a while. Part of it is because I'm excited about many small victories that have piled up over the last few months and I see them coming at an accelerated pace. Part of it is because I'm just wanting to "keep it real, Dawg."
So like Randy Jackson used to ask on American Idol, are you in it to win it?

Please say Yes. ~✰~

Michael Lives! (Gerber, that is)

Michael's the one on the left.
My wife says I'm the cutie on the right.

Less than 24 hours after the airwaves lit up our lives with the news of Michael Jackson's death, I was in a room full of business owners and entrepreneurs that not only DIDN'T discuss "the gloved one," they were all optimistic about their business opportunities, they were sharing ideas and they were making plans to not only GROW but to handle the growth they were already experiencing!

The AUDACITY! Grow. NOW? During this time of fiscal, economic and moon-walk-disappearing calamity? I ran to the Sheraton's lobby in search of a TV so we could see how distraught the world was about the King of Pop's passing. But sadly—rudely, almost—they were not showing the story so I shuffled back to my plaid Sheraton chair and skinny conference table stocked with mints, cold water, cheap pens and small hotel note pads and began sizing up this sharp-dressed man in the back of the room who wore a blue suit, matching fedora, cuff links and...BROWN* shoes.

He knew everyone and everyone was happy to see him but I thought this grey-bearded gentlemen was simply paying homage to MJ by wearing the fedora and maybe (hopefully) was going to juggle flaming bowling balls at the intermission. But that was not why the man in the blue fedora and brown shoes was there. (Maybe it's a "Michael thing" but big things do come in small packages.)

You would have never dreamt that such a powerful force of nature could be contained in such a diminutive stature. But Michael E. Gerber of "E-Myth" fame is a powerful force indeed. During our 2.5 hours together, we discussed the most important question you and I must answer if we are to not only succeed in our business endeavors but enjoy the journey along the way: "What is the meaning of my business?"

Can you answer that? Right now? If I woke you from a deep 2 AM slumber would it be propelled from your lips?

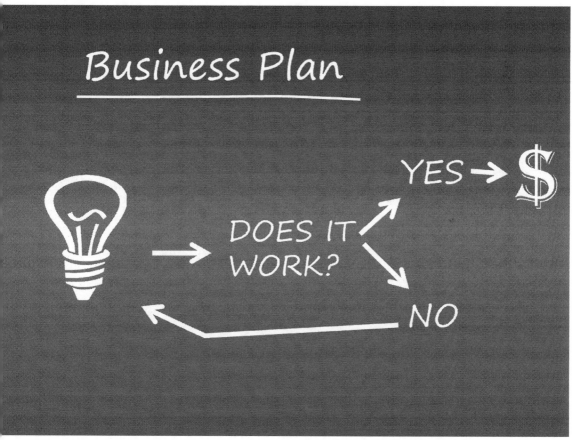

The meaning of my business is to make your business grow by helping you appreciate, understand and internalize the value you provide the world and to charge accordingly. Then we focus on the three areas that Michael teaches must be mastered to build and operate a successful business:

1) **Entrepreneurship** 2) **Management** 3) **Technician**

Technicians are usually those that start—and crash— a business because they do not understand systems, direct response marketing with strong calls to action and the importance of relationships, connecting and persuasion.

Entrepreneurs are the big dreamers and inventors of the end product, but they need the **managers** to create and supervise the processes and systems that are operated by technicians.

It's a dance that has been mastered by the likes of Ray Kroc. His business enables billions of food-like items to be served on time around the world by a teen-aged, hormone-raging work force that turns over 300% a year.

But that's not the most interesting tidbit about Ray Kroc. The most interesting fact is that Ray Kroc never worked in a McDonald's. He stayed outside the business to work on it instead of in it. He created systems that guaranteed success despite—and in spite of—the staff. And to this day, McDonald's franchise owners are forbidden by their contract to work in their own stores.

Would you like to have that kind of freedom and success? Answer the first question, "What is the meaning of my business?" Once you know that "the student will be ready and the teacher will appear." ~✶~

*Michael wore brown shoes because he forgot his black shoes when he packed to come see me and he thought he'd look less conspicuous wearing brown shoes instead of no shoes. It's good to know he's human like the all of us.

Money or Excuses

You have two choices in business and in life:
1. Make Money
2. Make (and accept) Excuses

They are mutually exclusive. Making money requires daily effort and focus. Excuses and alibis can last a lifetime, if you call a life full of excuses living.

Common excuses include…

- "My parents were (insert lame excuse, i.e. divorced, alcoholics, blue collar, white collar, inattentive,...). That's why I'm this way."
- "I grew up on the wrong side of the tracks."
- "My sibling got all the love and attention and new toys and clothes and brains and good looks and all the dates in high school."
- "There's too much competition."
- "I can't compete with India and China."
- "I don't know how to sell."
- "My boss is a jerk."
- "My company won't pay for any training."

- "My company won't pay for my cell phone."
- "Customers lie."
- "Prospects lie."
- "When the upgrade comes out I'll really be able to sell."
- "I'm not good at writing."
- "I'm not good at speaking."
- "I'm not technical."
- "I'm not good with numbers."
- "I have ADD."
- "I never finished college."
- "This whole 'social media' thing confuses me."
- "I'm too old / I'm too young."
- "I'm too white / black / brown / yellow."
- "I'm too fat / skinny."
- "When the kids are older..."
- "After the game I'll get around to it."
- "I've been in the industry 5-10-15-20 years." Translation "I'm so full of myself and complacent and arrogant and lazy that I'm now coasting and everyone on planet EARTH should bow to me and give me their business."
- "I'll think it over." AHHHHHHHHH!!
- "We've just always done it that way."
- "Let me run it by my manager."
- "Boy, you're sure proud of your stuff."
- "I can't attend training that early in the morning."
- "We didn't budget for that."
- "As soon as my show is over I'll get around to it."

Business is Selling and Selling is a zero-sum game. To the victor goes 100% of the prize. That's why professional sales people—the top 4%—make 56 times more money than the bottom 96%.

It's not because they are 56 times better. It's because they are consistently at least 1% (or .01 seconds) better, and that's enough to win gold. (Just ask that dude who could have been the most famous swimmer of the '08 Olympics if he would have finished strong and beaten Michael Phelps.)

What's your excuse for not achieving the goals you set for yourself last New Year's Day when you swore this year was going to be different? It's not too late to make it so. Even if you're reading this on New Year's Eve, you are finishing this year strong by working on yourself and your business so you can leap into next year with a renewed vigor, vitality and verve that you haven't felt since you were 16 and that special you-know-who finally called the house to see what you were doing this weekend.

You can feel 16 years old again—but with better judgment and less acne—but you must take action.

You are stronger, smarter and more capable than you think you are.
Start doing.
Start doing a lot of things.
Start doing the little things.
Start working towards the bigger things.
Start eliminating excuses and start living the life you were meant to live.

All the money and success and satisfaction and significance is out there just waiting for you to start stopping making excuses and start starting.

You can do it. ~☆~

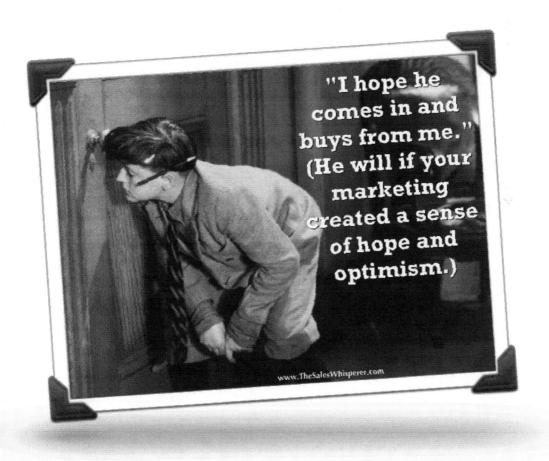

Temporary Braces. Permanent Support.

Jake's Braces Are Off

After almost two years my oldest got his braces off in August 2013 and you can see he, and my sister, Rachel, are quite happy about it. But did you know that two years of brute force is not enough to create lasting results? Today orthodontists install a small wire behind the teeth as a permanent retainer to ensure the results stick, which is just like your marketing efforts: just because you put a lot of time, money and effort into them, doesn't mean it will last forever.

That's why big brands like McDonald's regularly change everything from their slogans—"I'm lovin' it" vs. "What we're made of"—to their packaging to their cross-promotions—NASCAR in 2008, the NFL in 2012—to their celebrity spokespeople—Michael Jordan, Kobe Bryant, Lary Bird, Justin Timberlake.

What are you doing differently today to stay top-of-mind in your market? How are you reinforcing your business and yourself, which is probably one in the same, so you continue to grow and thrive?

In the next 12 months I encourage you to:

Write a book. (Jay Baer has a great SlideShare, "25 Secrets: How I Wrote and Marketed a New York Times Bestselling Business Book.") My first two books were self-published on Amazon's CreateSpace.com. It costs me less than $9 to print a 671 page book on Infusionsoft that I sell for $50 and it's the same price whether I print 1,000 or just one. Since going to print in September of 2012 I have made at least two sales per month ($299 to $2,000 up front and $99 to $299/mo) every month because "I'm the guy that wrote the book." That doesn't include the supplemental business in the way of web design, copywriting, consulting, etc. that I've earned from those clients that purchased Infusionsoft from me.

Start a podcast. (Pat Flynn, whom I met for lunch in August in San Diego, has a great tutorial, How To Start a Podcast.) Call Recorder is a $30 program that lets you record Skype calls on a Mac. Audacity is a free program. Strip out the audio and upload it to a free site like Podbean.com or an inexpensive site like LibSyn.com and you have a podcast.

Do more **videos** and have more **fun** in your marketing like PooPouri does on YouTube. I started with a $70 HD Logitech webcam from Sam's Club and moved up from there once I got comfortable. Those videos are still on my YouTube channel and making me money every day.

Redesign your website with conversions in mind. This can be daunting but it needs to happen every 2-3 years. That's why I started with Wordpress and now I have a professional team to help. Still, for five years, I did it on my own with the help of a full time virtual assistant in The Philippines.

Hire an assistant. I know you think you may not be able to afford help but if you are to grow and have time to enjoy the growth there a lot of little things you need to stop doing. I hired my virtual assistant years before I was 100% on my own. I hired my local assistant six month before I went on my own. Both helped me make a smoother transition into being a full time business owner. They'll free up your mind so you can dream bigger dreams and achiever bigger goals.

Run **contests** on social media.

Run **paid ads,** including **Retargeting,** on Google, LinkedIn and/or Facebook. You can spend as little as $10 per day to see if it can work for you. It may not be ideal to just jump right in, but most entrepreneurs only learn that way. Mastering how to drive paid traffic can eliminate the "feast or famine" in your small, medium or large businesses.

If you're still feeling froggy after all of this, make sure you are sending an **e-newsletter** at least monthly if not weekly.

Send a **printed newsletter** at least quarterly if not monthly.

Host a live **webinar** or training series that runs at least monthly.

Launch a **membership site** (contact me about iMember360 or AccessAlly) and join and/or start your own **mastermind**.

The key here is to commit to growth and stop "dabbling" around the edges of being a great marketer and sales professional by committing to growth, no matter what.

Along those lines I uploaded "12.9 Benefits of Being Committed To Growth" to SlideShare. You can view it for free at the following URL, **http://bit.ly/129growth**.

Remember, excuses last forever but the formula for success is permanent support via my Six D's: Daily Discipline Done Diligently Determines Destiny. ~✶~

Do Successful People Ever Stop Learning?

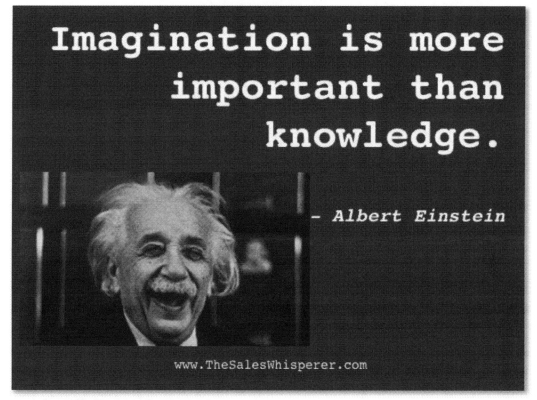

The kids are back in school as I write this (Aug 2013). I sat in an extra long line to drop Jake and Matthew off at high school as they started their Junior and Sophomore years, respectively. Sitting in that extra long line gave me plenty of time to ponder where this idea of taking three months off of learning came from. Oh, yeah: our farming, agrarian, horse-riding, straw-chewing great-great-great-great grandparents. "Ethel, get the chitlins up. Time to milk the cows and harvest the wheat and slop the pigs!" (With three teenagers and 3.5 siblings on their heels, I sometimes think I live in a pig pen but I've never had them slop pigs and I don't know too many people that have. Do you?)

Success in school, and life, requires constant learning. In Malcolm Gladwell's book, "Outliers: The Story of Success," he talks about the Knowledge Is Power Program (KIPP) in the Bronx, where kids go to school on Saturdays, in the Summer and for longer days during the school year. The result? By the end of 8th grade, 84% of students are performing at or above grade level, compared to 16% for the district schools in the area.

Think of the five most successful people you know. What do they have in common? I can guarantee you they are always working on their education and improving their skills. They are attending conferences and workshops. They are hiring experts to train them and their teams and implement better processes in their businesses and life. They are growing.

What are you doing to grow? What books are you reading? (Thanks for reading this book. It's a great start.) What podcasts are you listening to? (May I recommend a good one www.TheSalesPodcast.com? :-) What conferences are you attending? With whom are you masterminding? To help you grow I gave you a link to "12.9 Benefits of Being Committed To Growth." Now I'll share "The 7.9 Fundamentals of Growth"— **http://bit.ly/79fungrow**.

Spend time on both of those presentations and on all of links found in the Resources section at the back of the book. I provide them because if you think your "formal education" is all you need to get you where you want to go, you are in for a surprise. You and I have to grab the bull by the horns (the other side is too gross) and take control of our own destinies by continuing to educate ourselves and by associating with people that make us stretch.

It's worth the effort. Happy Learning. ~*~

Prospects Tell You How To Sell To Them

Ever notice how the words "learn" and "earn" have the word "ear" in them? It's simple and obvious, right? But it didn't really dawn on me until a few years ago. (Mind like a steel trap. Nothing gets in or out.)

We've all heard the saying, "You have two ears and one mouth: Use them proportionately." But we also hear, "You're so good with people. You could sell plastic surgery to Joan Rivers. You should be in sales."

So which is it? To be a great salesperson, do we listen or talk? Observe or schmooze? Ponder or prescribe?

Obviously the answer is the front half of all three questions, but that's not how we're taught. We're taught to give long presentations, detailed demonstrations and review bloated brochures. The sales people we see on TV are all smooth talkers, fancy dressers, quick-witted CLOSERS ready to buy you a drink, a round of golf or the meal of your life if you'll just sign on the bottom line and take delivery by the end of the month.

Sales Pros know nothing could be further from the truth. People buy when they are ready to buy. They get ready to buy through research, analysis, a gut feeling and/or a recommendation. They buy to scratch an itch, to fill a void, to stop a pain or to bring pleasure. How they do all of the above depends on their personality, their needs, their desires and their current situation, all of which can change from year to year and even month to month. The only way you'll know is to observe everything they do and say, how they say it, how long it takes for them to say it, and the words they use to say it.

You must observe their surroundings and attire, their demeanor, even their personal grooming and accessories, or lack thereof. Additionally, during your interaction with them, whether it be a few minutes or a few months, notice if any of the above changes suddenly or drastically. If they are animated when they speak, do they suddenly withdraw? If they are normally dressed in a conservative manner, do they arrive for a meeting in flashier or more stylish clothing? Are they typically quite sure of themselves and confident but cannot make eye contact when you ask a particular question?

Understanding the verbal and non-verbal queues people provide is critical to your sales success. It's a major tenant of the #1 sales trait of great sales people, which is having empathy. That's why I interviewed Barbara Metzger of Max Productivity. She's an expert in personality assessments, which are like Rosetta Stone for connecting with people. After 30 years Barbara knows what she is talking about and she answered every question I threw at her during our 40+ minutes together (**TheSalesWhisperer.com/session14**).

Picking up on these personality types was the most difficult skill for me to learn when I began treating selling as a profession and a career. To this day I continue to work on better ways to detect a person's buying style so I can do a better job of engaging with them. It's like a massage therapist asking you if you have any injuries or areas you'd like him to focus on, except we can't always come out and ask, "Tell me how to sell you." Or can we?

After all these years of selling I've learned that whomever is asking the questions is in control. Watch your favorite police officer or attorney show to see what I mean. The cop corners the suspect and asks where she was at 10:15 PM last night and the suspect has to answer. Ditto for the school teacher asking his class to name the capitals of all 50 states or the difficult prospect asking you to prove to her why your stuff is better, and if it's compatible with her current software, and if it has a better warranty, more options, faster delivery, better documentation and support, and if it comes in purple.

To keep this from happening—and to keep you in control of every situation—you need to do your homework ahead of time and you need an Agenda for every meeting. Having and following a mutually-agreed upon Agenda will help you connect and convert more prospects—even the tough ones—even if you can't get good answers to your homework questions.

In a nutshell, you are serving notice, in a polite but firm way, that you are not setting an appointment with the prospect to show up and throw up. You are meeting with them to see if there is a fit for your two companies to work together. You request open and honest communication and anyone from either party may end the meeting at any time for any reason. (You should see the shoulders relax, the eyes come up from the smartphones and people lean in when you drop that little kitty in the punch bowl.)

Next, you let them know that you are going to have a lot of questions about their current situation and that, in the interest of time, they may want to jot down a few for you. Finally, you inform them that after getting a better feel for their situation, if you think you can help them you will outline your recommendations and you ask them to conclude the meeting with a firm answer on how they would like to proceed.

I have used this Agenda to sell millions of dollars of hardware, software and services to clients such as Google, Dell, Sprint and the local owner of a water purification company. It can work for you and it is outlined in great detail at **TheSalesAgenda.com**.

There are two types of sales:
1. The easy ones.
2. And those you don't get.

This Agenda makes a lot more of them easy. ~*~

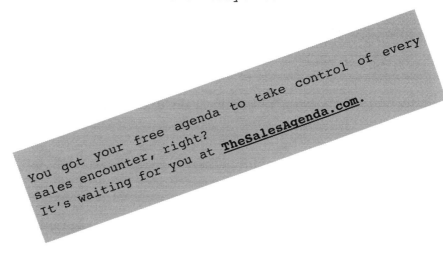

You got your free agenda to take control of every sales encounter, right? It's waiting for you at **TheSalesAgenda.com**.

Entertain To Not Be a Pain

All Work & No Play Is Making You—And Your Marketing—Dull

Just 33.3% of our lives (8 hours out of 24) should be spent on work, according to the Man Upstairs, who worked 6 days a week, by the way. (So much for that 21-hour work week the French want us follow, right?).

14.3% of our days (1 day a week), should be spent resting 100% of the time, which is known as the Sabbath, which is when everyone is talking trash in their Fantasy Football leagues. (Is that why God rested on the 7th day: To watch football? I know on the 8th day he made Texas...but I digress.)

If 66.6% of your work days should be focused on something other than work, why is 100% of your marketing formal, uninspired, jargon-filled blah that is all work and no play? That type of marketing at best falls on deaf ears and at worst backfires and causes you to actually lose that potential client forever.

(Paying to lose clients? "Whatchoo talkin 'bout Willis?")
It's sad and crazy but true.

We all hear how hard it is to attract, capture and retain the attention of people today, but Fantasy Football has no problem attracting a lot of attention from a third of North America.

"But, Wes, that's FOOTBALL. It's entertainment. It's what people do in order to take their minds off of work. Of course it has their attention." People already have their minds OFF of work AT work. So why not meet them where they are?

"Ahhh, sounds good, Wes...but how do I do that?" I thought you'd never ask. As always, it starts with the headline:

- Your Dentist Wants You To Win Your Fantasy Football League
- Your Fantasy Football Or Your Life. (Why Choose? ACME Insurance Helps You Get Both Covered. Call For Details.)
- Get Your Back—And Your Fantasy Football—Straightened Out At ACME Chiropractic. Call For Details.

"Wes, how the heck can a dentist help with Fantasy Football?" Simple. There are Fantasy Football subscription services for $29.95. Maybe, to get more new patients in during the summer, the dentist or chiropractor offers a subscription to all new patients that come in between June and August.

Ditto for the life insurance agent.

"But, Wes, I don't make much money. I sell a little gizmo for just $29.95."

Ok. Then buy the subscription and create a private Facebook Group that only new clients can access and you provide the tips and suggestions you find on the service and answer questions from your new clients.

Total Cost: $29.95
Engagement With Clients: Up 100—10,000%
Total Value: Priceless

Or throw a Fantasy Football draft party, contact 10-20 local businesses and get them to kick in $50-$100 each as sponsors so you buy chips and snacks and drinks and rent some tables and chairs or find a local sports bar or restaurant with Wi-Fi and say "I want to bring in 20-30-50 people for a draft night. Can I get a discount on food and drinks and a private room?"

Run this promotion all summer, "Anyone that purchases in June, July and August gets invited to the draft party." Get $100-$2,000 contributed from local sponsors so you pay nothing other than a little sweat equity and some time planning the promotion and getting the word out.

It would help if you or someone in your company was a Fantasy Football fan so you can really get into it. If so, you found a way to not only subsidize your hobby but you also found a way to connect with an extra 10 or 100 or 1,000 prospects and new clients in a way that gets their attention.

Total Cost: $29.95
Engagement With Clients: Up 100—10,000%
Total Value: Priceless

"But, Wes, it's so hard...and I don't like Fantasy Football and neither do my clients."

Marketing yourself and your business is your #1 job. Accept that fact or accept mediocrity. (Don't shoot the messenger.) Put on your thinking cap to figure out how to apply this Fantasy Football party idea to other prospects.

If you service an older clientele, maybe you sponsor a BINGO night or a big band night or build it around the Kentucky Derby and have a viewing party or tie it to bird-watching if that is big in your area. Whatever you link your event to doesn't matter. Just make sure it resonates with your clients and prospects so you can cut through the clutter and get their attention.

It's ok to have fun in business and in life and since your business is your life, it's smart business to have fun doing both at the same time.

Do it now before your competition does. Then leave a comment on my site or send me an email letting me know your results.

Are you smiling, yet? ~✷~

"_____ Before Social Media."

Jay Baer Is On
The Sales Whisperer®
Podcast, Session 15.

@jaybaer

TheSalesWhisperer.com/session15

Jay Baer is an NYT best-selling author, hype-free social media and marketing consultant and he speaks more than 75 times a year to groups as large as 5,000. He has started five multi-million dollar companies, consulted for 30 of the Fortune 500 and his blog is the #1 content marketing blog in the world.

On August 16th, 2013, this social media guru was a guest on my podcast—**TheSalesWhisperer.com/session15**—and what he recommended about social media was quite shocking.

You'd think he'd be "all social media all the time." The reality is you first need to have a good product. "Social media isn't going to patch up your wounds. If your company sucks, Twitter is the least of your worries. Companies that are great at social media are usually great companies."

Once you have a great company, start a blog. (See the "Communication Celebration (Word Up Wordpress") chapter.) The blog serves as your hub, your home plate, the center of your marketing universe. Social media sites are the spokes on the wheel that attract traffic and bring those visitors, those browsers, those people back to your site.

Which brings us to Jay's main point. "If you're not **great at email,** you have no business doing social. If you can't send out one great thing a week or build a nurturing sequence inside (your email client,) why would you want to tackle something that happens in real time?"

Have you bitten off more than you can chew? Have you taken the "all social media all the time" hype to the detriment of your product and your company? Does email marketing confuse you? Does the thought of being great wear you out?

You're not alone.

We all get tired.

The good news is, these thoughts and obstacles are just as exhausting and tiring to your competitors.

The great news is you only have to be 1% better than them to win 100% of the business.

But you have to be better at the things that matter. ~*~

Your Next Step Is Obvious—If You're Willing To Do The Analysis

"It requires a very unusual mind to undertake the analysis of the obvious." ~Alfred North Whitehead

"Wes, it's not obvious why you opened with that quote...nor why you included it here."

Anything we want to improve needs to be analyzed, studied and broken down into its components to identify bottlenecks and areas for improvement. This is true of your golf swing, how McDonald's delivers a preservatives-filled glob of mystery meat and how you create your own profit-producing People, Process, Product, to borrow a line from Marcus Lemonis.

You must take the time to study the "obvious" pieces of your business in order to improve.

"But, Wes, I know my business like I know the back of my hand."

Really? When was the last time you really looked at the back of your hand? (Why are you studying your hand when you need to study your business?)

Since 2008 I've personally sat down with over 750 small business owners, sales people, and entrepreneurs during in-depth sessions to help them figure out how to best grow their sales.

Out of all of those sessions, maybe 5 or 6 could answer even a few detailed questions such as:

- How many dials of the phone does it take to make an appointment?
- How many appointments are kept?
- How many kept appointments turn into a quote or proposal?
- How many quotes turn into a sale?
- How many sales turn into repeat orders?
- How many clients provide referrals and testimonials?
- How many leads did you capture last month?
- What was the most effective lead- generation tool you employed over the last 30-60-180 days?
- What was the best converting headline of your free report or MP3 or landing page?
- What are your top 3 sources for web traffic and how are they trending over the last quarter?

By analyzing the obvious, Dell cut forecast errors 300% and reduced freight and manufacturing costs by 30% in 2010. By analyzing the obvious, Apple has crippled its competitors during past Christmas seasons and during the release of new products by gobbling up capacity in everything from air freight to touch screens.

"But, Wes, I'm not a multi-billion dollar Fortune 50 company. I'm just little ol' me, trying to grow enough to get some sleep at night and afford a family vacation from time to time." All the more reason to buckle down, take a step back then zoom in on your business because "small levers swing big doors."

Oh, yeah. I almost forgot. An orthodontist automated the delivery of greeting cards and thoughtful gifts during the course of a patient's treatment and now takes 42 vacation days a year instead of 5 after three years of focusing on the obvious and automating it. (Is an orthodontist small enough for you? What's that? You don't have the degrees and credentials of an orthodontist? Ok. A church financial guy $80,000 in debt is now running a $2.1 million business that is now an Inc. 500 Award winner and is adding to his business ventures. **TheSalesWhisperer.com/session9**. No more excuses.)

There are people in your industry working less and earning more than you right now. To rub salt into the wound: they are not as smart, not as dedicated and not as caring as you are.

"Wes, I KNOW and it's driving my CRAZY! It's just not fair."

You're 100% right. What are you going to do about it?

You can keep working hard with a caring, dedicated, martyrdom attitude that may eventually pay off in the long run...Or you can care enough to stop a moment to think things through, seek outside expertise where needed and do what it takes to truly understand your business, what it will take to thrive and finally get paid what you're worth.

It's obvious you're not earning to your full potential isn't it? Now what are you going to do about it? ~*~

Mind Mastery or Minutiae?

Every day—literally, EVERY DAY—I speak to an aspiring or struggling sales manager, entrepreneur, business owner and/or sales person who asks for that one nugget, that latest tip or trick to help them overcome their most recent hurdle or obstacle, thinking that's all they need to have smooth sailing ahead.

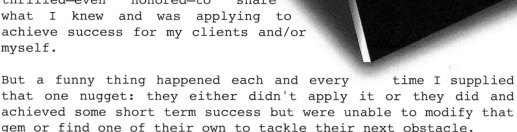

And for many years I was happy, thrilled—even honored—to share what I knew and was applying to achieve success for my clients and/or myself.

But a funny thing happened each and every time I supplied that one nugget: they either didn't apply it or they did and achieved some short term success but were unable to modify that gem or find one of their own to tackle their next obstacle.

After experiencing this *failure to execute* bring clients of all ages, in dozens of industries, across five continents to their knees, I finally realized external stuff will always happen. It's called entropy. I learned all about it in my physics and thermodynamics courses at USAFA and Texas A&M. (After 26 years I'm glad I can use that little nugget of a word somewhere.)

Entropy—the tendency of everything in the universe to move towards disorder / thermodynamic equilibrium—applies to cars and planets and stars and laptop computers and GoDaddy servers and our DVRs at home, the GPS in our cars and our own thinking.

Which is why the nuggets, gems, tips, tricks and tactics are the proverbial fish, and if I only provide those to you it will help you eat today, but not help you learn how to fish and feed yourself forever.

To teach you how to fish in business, I need to help you learn to master your own thinking and belief systems because if you think…

- you're too old;
- you're too young;
- the world is out to get you;
- you're not smart enough;

- you need to go to college;
- you're not tall enough;
- you need to be a man;
- you need to be a woman;
- you need a new computer/car/office;
- you need (insert nasally, whiny excuse)...

...Then you suffer from STINKIN' THINKIN'.

You and I didn't suffer from this as kids. The world was our animal cracker. (I didn't like oysters until I could wash them down with a cold beer, which is around 10 or 11 in South Louisiana! :-)

When we were young we were going to be policeman, firemen, teachers, doctors, astronauts and professional athletes all at the same time.

We wore superhero underwear, believed in happily-ever-after and just knew we could fly (but didn't jump off the roof because we didn't want to upset our parents, who lost that ability when stinkin' thinkin' took over some time in the far distant past.) :-(

It's time to get rid of that stinkin' thinkin'.

It's time to believe you have the power to speak worlds into existence. (Read any Stephen King or John Grisham lately?) You can create your own world, but first you must think it into existence.

To build big you must think big. Once you have that big, clear(er) vision in your mind, you'll know what is (or what NEEDS) to be created, and you can begin in earnest to bring it into reality. This clarity of vision and purpose and commitment to action is how you turn obstacles into opportunities and turn challenges into reasons to excel.

If you need help, one of the best and most affordable ways to grow is to find a mastermind group. If you can't find a mastermind group, start one. If you think you can't, your stinkin' thinkin' is more powerful than you think.

Turn off the TV and Facebook and listen to free podcasts from people with positive messages. If you live on an island alone with no phone or internet access, swim to your nearest library or bookstore, and begin reading books on motivation by coaches, speakers and trainers that you like and resonate with you.

If you give negative thoughts less room and less time to infiltrate your brain, positive thoughts and better thinking will begin to fill that void.
"But, Wes, that motivational stuff doesn't last." Like Zig Ziglar said, "Neither does bathing. That's why I suggest you do it daily."

The best time to plant a tree is 20 years ago. The second best time is today. Ditto for better thinking.

On your marks. Get set. Start thinking better. ~*~

Hey, sidebar:

When was the last time you thought about what your prospect was thinking? I mean really followed the advice of Robert Collier who encouraged us to "enter the conversation already going on in your prospect's mind"?

When you're focused on the wants, fears, goals, and desires of your prospects and you're there to serve their needs instead of yours, you'll be shocked at how much easier the conversations— and the sales—become.

So follow the #1 Golden Rule by treating others the way you want to be treated.

Then you'll be able to live by the #2 Golden Rule, which is "Thou who hast the gold, maketh the rules."

Now go listen, learn, then earn.

Back to Basics?

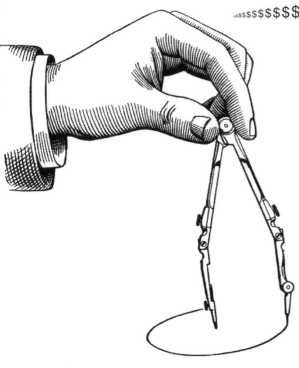

When the *fit hits the shan* we are told to "get back to basics." What does that mean? Go door-to-door? Put up billboards? Sponsor a Little League team?

When I started selling for a network marketing company in 1994, we didn't have cell phones or text messaging or social media. I used a PC at work but it wasn't until late 1995 that I had a home email address. There was no blogging, caller ID or "sales and marketing automation." YouTube was 11 years from being invented, iPhones were 13 years from being released and "search engine optimization" was still over three years away from being mentioned by John Audette and Bruce Clay, which was one year before Google came into being.

If an "old timer" like me "gets back to basics," does that mean I unplug, place a big ad in the Yellow Pages and start smiling and dialing?

Maybe those basics are too far back so let's jump ahead 10 years to 2004 when real estate was booming, Zuckerberg was a 19-year old Harvard student and MySpace was the cool place to get social. Those were some basic times, right?

What's that? That was before the financial bubble burst? So those "new-old" basics don't work anymore? We need some "new-new" basics now? How do you know? Do you know what they are or where to find them or how to recognize them when you do find the new-new basics? Will you know how to best apply them to grow your own sales? Are you willing to bet the future of your business on it?

On January 1, 2019, I'll enter my 25th year of being in sales and marketing. (I began with a direct marketing company while still in the Air Force.)

To put that into perspective, I began learning how connect with and persuade people when:

- Clinton was still impressing interns.

- The Dow was at 3,750.
- Ace Of Base topped the Billboard charts and
- We learned that "life was like a box of chocolates."

For 25 years I've been learning from Tom Hopkins, Zig Ziglar, Tony Robbins, Brian Tracy, Dan Kennedy, Napoleon Hill, et al. (Yeah, yeah. I know those guys had been around a while but the Air Force wasn't concerned about us thinking or growing rich. Nor did they care about us walking on hot coals.)

Despite having a guaranteed career laid out for me, getting paid according to my effort and production vs. tenure was what motivated me, as it is for all entrepreneurs. In 1997, with a wife, a baby and another on the way I left that guaranteed career for a commission sales job and I've been growing and helping others do the same ever since. The basics of sales and marketing have changed.

"Wes, are you saying gripping-and-grinning and Yellow Page ads and fish bowls at restaurants and storing 1,000 business cards in my desk drawer with a rubber band around them are no longer effective ways to grow a business?"

Maybe.

"Wes, I'm hip and current. I know all about FaceTube and YouBook and Twitteragram and LinkedTerest and PinSpace. I even blogged once last year. I got this new stuff down to a science degree or something."

That's good to hear. You probably have all the business you need. No reason to read further.

However, if you are still scratching your head about how to minimize your efforts and maximize your results, look inward to see if you have neglected your tried-and-true basics that made you who you are and go back to them. Then look outward to find someone still making it happen and learn from them so you can master and apply the new basics.

What makes you unique will always be the cornerstone of your business. How you tell the world and help the world tell your story is what is changing. Is your continued success worth the effort to find those leading by example, to learn from them and apply what they learn? You bet it is.

The best help will not be cheap. But neither are you. And neither are your best clients, whom you need to reach more persuasively, consistently, and effectively than ever because we're frazzled and exhausted.

If, after pausing to read this section, you're not going back to something you love to do, but you have no choice and you must do it to keep the lights on, take a closer at your basics. You'll know what you must do. ~*~

Hey, sidebar:

Have you heard the saying by the original "Mad Man" David Ogilvy that you can't save souls in an empty church?

Greg and Julie Alexander were living that empty church feeling. They're not preachers but they do have a non-profit ministry that helps struggling married couples get through their tough times and grow closer together.

Despite being great speakers with a compelling story they were struggling to get the numbers they needed to grow their ministry. Fortunately for them they came to speak at the Ontario Convention Center here in Southern California a couple years ago, which is about an hour from me so I drove up to see them and give them some coaching on how to close from the stage.

We had about 90 minutes before they were set to speak to about 200 attendees and I knew right away what their Achilles heel was so we went to work.

To their credit, Greg and Julie were 100% coachable and put their trust in me. Instead of passing out expensive, typical, and boring mini-brochures I had them put them away and simply go with the "executive decision" close. That's where Greg looks sheepishly at Julie—it works if you're alone as well—and says near the end of the talk "Julie is going to kill me, but you've been a great audience and we're running out of time so I'm going to make an executive decision."

You then offer to give a bonus session or webinar or guide, etc. A valuable bonus that you weren't planning on doing, which is why you don't have any order forms or text messaging short code or website for them to go to. You just have them write their name and email on a piece of paper and hand it to them.

Yes, it requires a little data entry but you can see the results…

The Hard Lessons of the Hardheaded

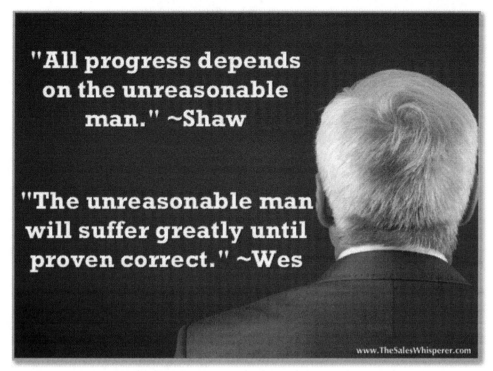

"All progress depends on the unreasonable man." ~Shaw

"The unreasonable man will suffer greatly until proven correct." ~Wes

www.TheSalesWhisperer.com

The beauty of being an entrepreneur is that you get to prove to everyone that you're not crazy. That you know what you're doing. That you know best.

That is, unless you're wrong.

In 1903 George Bernard Shaw wrote his Maxims for Revolutionists. #124 was "The reasonable man adapts himself to the world: the unreasonable one persists in trying to adapt the world to himself. Therefore all progress depends on the unreasonable man."

Was Shaw talking about entrepreneurs?

I think so, since entrepreneurs create revolutions in the marketplace. Come to think of it, aren't all actual revolutions made possible by entrepreneurs? Certainly Twitter made some of the uprisings in the Middle East possible. Is a political leader who encourages his fellow citizens to stand up for their beliefs an entrepreneur? I think so.

But history is written by the victorious. Political entrepreneurs that aren't quite good enough end up back home working in the family septic tank business or dead, depending on the opponent.

Business entrepreneurs that aren't quite good enough end up back home working in a cubicle and dead broke, and maybe wishing they were dead. (But real entrepreneurs bounce back. It's what we do because "you can't keep a good man down." Or a good woman for that matter.)
But the same pigheaded determination that keeps an entrepreneur going against all odds is the same trait that created the "it's lonely at the top" adage.

Stubborn entrepreneurs may not seek council or listen to the advice of those that have gone before. They see themselves as different and unique and they are right, but they do not realize so is every other achieving, striving, focused entrepreneur.

This feeling of "the world is out to get me" and "I'm a sea of sanity in a world of morons" and "in the land of the blind the one-eyed man is king" can and does lead to great stretches of angst, worry, doubt, fear and suffering.

But we're told "NO PAIN NO GAIN" so we soldier on, not realizing there are others just like us in our own home towns— maybe even our own neighborhoods—toiling away as an unreasonable entrepreneur so determined to make the world a better place and to build a better mousetrap that they do not venture out to a Chamber of Commerce mixer or neighborhood block party or free S.C.O.R.E. workshop to realize there are other "odd balls" like us nearby that can help us see our blind spots, provide an encouraging word or bounce an idea off of from time to time.

Suffering and doing without for a loved one or a worthy cause is admirable. Doing it because it's the only thing you know how to do is stupid. (Sure, I could've said silly or foolish or unwise, but you and I don't have time to mince words. Only the sensitive and the stupid do that, right?)

You, the hardheaded entrepreneur slaying

dragons and windmills and government red tape and slothful, entitled employees and lying vendors are not alone. And like my dad always says, "If you think you're desperate, you are." Continue moving forward with vim and vigor. Remain hard-headed and unreasonable and determined. If you'd like to interact with me and other motivated entrepreneurs for free, head on over to our private group at **TheImplementors.com**.

Unless you're too hardheaded. ~*~

Hey, sidebar:

People close to you won't always "get" you, your vision, your optimism, your fear of the status quo, your dread of the cubicle and the same daily commute for 30 years, your willingness to spend 80 hours to fix a process that'll save just 18 seconds, but 18 people on your staff do it 18 times per day. (For the record, that's 486 minutes, or 8.1 hours, per week, which means you'll have a positive ROI on your efforts in less than 10 weeks.)

Small hinges swing big doors, and you know where the hinges are needed and the doors that need to be opened faster, wider, and more smoothly.

Now go open something.

The Conflicting Role of Hope

Hope is a poor sales strategy. Hope is the key to great marketing.

Oh the dichotomy of growing a business.

Sales people are notorious hopers.

They hope they can smooth talk their way in to see the boss. They hope the right words will pop into their heads at the moment of truth. They hope they'll make the big sale, hit their numbers, get a promotion, win awards and be cheered and respected by the Academy of Sales and statues will be erected in their honor.

"Hopium" is an addictive, deadly drug that seduces every sales person at some point in their career.

Like ridding yourself of unwanted girth around the midsection, the only cure for "hopium" is daily discipline. (Remember D.D.D.D.D.D.: Daily Discipline Done Diligently Determines Destiny?)

This discipline applies to your daily sales activities, which include making the appropriate number of prospecting calls, having sufficient conversations with decision makers, conducting demonstrations and submitting enough winning proposals to guarantee you succeed in sales.

This discipline also applies to your daily marketing activities. However, in your marketing you MUST include and instill a healthy dose of hope and optimism in the minds of your readers and prospects to move them into taking action.

Since 1855 inventors have hoped their better mousetrap would make them rich. (The truth behind the actual date and actual author will be the subject of another letter.) Are your words strong enough to move people today, let alone centuries from now?

Do you know they're strong enough or do you hope they are?

If you'd like to remove all doubt, join your peers—professional salespeople, sales managers, business owners and entrepreneurs— who hang out and support one another at **TheImplementors.com**.

You'll make friends, gain needed insight, and the motivation, confidence, and support to actually implement them to produce the growth you've been seeking.

I hope to see you then. ~*~

> *"We had a 74% opt-in from a 180-person audience… In the past we might get 3-4 names. Now we can help these people.*
>
> **~Greg & Julie Alexander**
> **The Alexander House**

Your TedX Right Angle Talk

TED's tagline is "Ideas worth spreading."

On Nov 16th, 2013 the fine folks at TEDX Temecula arranged a series of TED talks around the concept of "The Next Stage."

Along those lines they asked me to spread some ideas on what's next in sales. I wrote it as a blog post first to fine tune my thinking and my message. **TheSalesWhisperer.com/tedx**

Doing things like this are good for you, me, all of us. It makes us stretch. It gets us out of our comfort zones. It makes us really think through and analyze the message we wish to convey, and it puts us front and center where we need to be as entrepreneurs, as sales leaders, and as thought leaders.

That last piece—thought leaders—is important. Your prospects need to see you as a well-rounded human being. They need to see you outside of where they "expect" to see you.

This type of "surprise sighting" is a pleasant way of making an impression on—and in—your marketplace. Speaking and getting involved in things that are not directly linked to your "day job" is a form of "right angle selling."

Right Angle Selling means rather than approaching your prospects directly to "take them on" and "overcome their objections" and engage in "psychological combat," you approach

in a less-hostile, less-confrontational manner, in a type of "flanking" maneuver.

You engage them in dialogue. You ask thoughtful questions. You present yourself as an interesting, professional human being and let them ask you, when they're ready, what it is you do "exactly."

In order to create these situations you must put yourself out there. But that's hard. For all of our lives we have been raised to not **toot our own horns.** You don't know how to stand out and get the attention of your prospective clients so you blend in. You "go along to get along." You realize it's rough to live by the adage that "if you haven't pissed someone off by noon you're not marketing." Which is why so many businesses fail.

It's tough to hear people say "Oh, you're in sales?" or "You're only in it for the money" or "What are you peddling this week?"

Granted, if people are responding to you like this you're doing something wrong, but in order to do things right you have to endure doing it wrong. (This book, and the Resources at the back, can help accelerate and shorten your learning curve.)

But you got into business because you had a business idea worth spreading. Maybe the idea was better dental care in your city or more affordable web design for small business owners or better child care for working parents. Whatever it is, go forth with passion and focus and intensity to spread that idea, to be known as the quality provider of whatever it is you do.

So when is your next talk? ~✱~

What Are You Selling For Valentine's Day?

(Sent mid-November, 2013)

Email Marketing Tip #20: Create an annual / evergreen email calendar to reuse every year to prime the pump for your marketing efforts.

I know what you're thinking: *"Valentine's Day? It's not even Thanksgiving and Wes is asking me what my Valentine's Day sale is going to be? I think he's hitting the spiked egg nog a little early this year."*

Yes, I am hitting the egg nog early this year. (Shannon actually brought some home just the other day.) But I haven't spiked it...yet. I promise.

I ask this question because you need to be thinking and planning your marketing campaigns weeks and even months ahead to build a successful, sustainable, enjoyable business that is a true asset to you and your family instead of some "Frankenstein business" that chains you to your desk for all eternity.

You have to make the time to get ahead of the madness, even if that means giving up some short term sales for long term stability.

"WHAT? Give up sales? On purpose? Now? Stop the madness!"

With Thanksgiving just 15 days away you can forget about doing any type of elaborate, memorable, effective promotion that both makes you money and solidifies your position as a vendor of value in the eyes of your marketplace if you haven't already laid the foundation for that launch.

You will be much better served to skip a Thanksgiving promotion and observe what your competition does and survey your clients and prospects to understand what they are looking for and what they need during this time of year so you can begin working on your Thanksgiving 2014 promotion.

It's like being in a band, which I was in waaaaay back in Junior High. The instructor told us if we messed up or got lost on a section of music to simply stop, look ahead to where we could comfortably rejoin and pick it up from there.

Under no circumstances were we to attempt to "catch up."

Imagine the chaos of having one saxophone, two trumpets, a clarinet and a french horn all trying to "catch up" while the rest of the band was on time.

The same is true with your business.

If you fell behind in your marketing - and it happens to all of us - take a moment to catch your breath. Look ahead to Christmas, New Year's, President's Day and Valentine's Day and ask yourself where can you hop in and do it right.

The good news is, once you have a solid promotion you can both use it again next year and, with minimal adjustments, apply it to another campaign later in the year.

Think about it. A sales event is a sales event. You choose the item you want to promote. Determine the discount or bundled offer. Set the time frame or quantity available at that price. Maybe give your best customers a heads-up or sneak peek or "early bird" chance to take advantage of the sale, and launch.

Measure the results then take your Valentine's Day **red-theme**, **make it green**, remove the heart's and Cupids, add some leprechauns and you have your St. Patrick's Day Sale. Make it red, white and blue and add pictures of families having a picnic and you have your 4th of July sale.

It really is that simple.

So if you find yourself behind this time of year take a moment to stop, look and listen. Maybe God is telling you to unplug and unwind a bit right now. Maybe catch up on some reading, watch your favorite movies, tend to that home-improvement project you've been putting off or play some games with the family.

Once you're calm and refreshed, pour yourself some egg nog, take note of what is working and what is not, write your New Year's goals early and get started on them now. Hiding or ignoring or rushing around to implement half-baked systems and promotions only hurts you.

Cut yourself some slack and hop in when you're ready and you'll be amazed at how much more thankful you'll be in 15 days...and 15 years. ~*~

TED Talks & Typos

On Saturday Nov 16, 2013, I was the closing presenter at TEDx Temecula...and I had a typo.

But only a friend in another state noticed the typo - at least he's the only one that said anything - and that was yesterday after sharing photos from the event. (What are the odds that the FIRST photo I shared captured the slide with the typo and I didn't catch it while making the presentation or sharing the photo?!)

Why do I tell you this? A few reasons.
One, to reassure you we're all human.
Two, to prove that most mistakes aren't fatal.
Three, to encourage you to enter the arena, step out on the field, get up on stage despite the risk of failures, large or small, real or perceived.

Why?

Because you're in business to grow and you need people to sell to in order to grow so you need to realize people don't do business with you for one of two reasons:
One: They haven't heard of you.
Two: They have.

The former problem is yours to resolve.
You need to put yourself out there now, not when you feel "ready," because you're never 100% ready. There will always be ~~typohs~~...~~tipoes~~...misspelled words.

I've been giving talks since I ran for student council in 1987 and played a Beastie Boys parody with my running mate in front of 647 teenage boys in our high school auditorium. (I didn't win but I still love the Beastie Boys.)

I've delivered keynotes to
- 400 hungover sales people in Vegas,
- 200 restless teenagers on a church retreat, and
- 1,200 fundraising attendees,

So one might say I was "ready" to deliver the TedX talk.

But I've never given a TED talk. I've never had to deliver an 18-minute talk that was this tight, this scripted, on this exact topic. (They assigned a theme for the entire day and we had to mold our message to that theme.)

I worked and re-worked this TEDx talk for 6 weeks. I wrote it then re-wrote it as a blog post (**TheSalesWhisperer.com/tedx**) to clarify my thinking, then created the presentation from my post.

I emailed the slide deck to our technical team and did a dry run the night before and printed my slides to review them the day of the talk and we all still missed the typo.

Is that a failure or a success that I was A) asked to be part of this TEDx talk, B) asked to be the "closer," and C) actually pulled it off?

That question is rhetorical.

This one is not: When is your next talk? ~✳~

P.S. As for the latter, take comfort in knowing that you repel to the same degree that you attract, so forget about those that aren't drawn to you and let them find someone else to scratch their itch. Besides, just one Justin Bieber video—"Baby" featuring Ludacris—has **9.4 million DISLIKES on nearly two BILLION views.**

So until 9.4 million people say they don't like what you're doing, I'd say you're pretty well liked. (And the "Biebs" seems to be weathering those numbers just fine.)

You Can Be Your New Car

Is it just me, or are you also **amazed** at how early in the year auto manufacturers release next year's models? You can buy a 2019 in August of 2018—or even February—with no problem.

Having been in sales for many years, I always sold what I had and only discussed the "new and improved" planned for next year's release if I was losing to a competitor and had to throw sand in the gears of my competitor.

But if BMW and Ford and Mercedes and Audi can show us their 2019 models in August of 2018, and Cadillac is showing their 2019 Escalade in October of 2018, why can't you and I present our new, future selves today, also?

So Sunday I did just that. I pulled out my (ashamedly-rarely-reviewed) goals for 2018 and reviewed them one last time before I threw them away and wrote my 2019 goals. THAT'S RIGHT. YOU HEARD ME. I WROTE MY 2019 GOALS ON AUGUST 24TH, 2018. TAKE THAT DETROIT!! TWO CAN PLAY AT THAT GAME! (But if there are three manufacturers in Detroit, should it be "four can play at that game?" Hmm...You get my point.)

And it was a great feeling. It's still a cool feeling as I've

WES IS RIGHT. NOW'S A GOOD TIME TO REBOOT AND REINVENT MYSELF.

been working towards those goals daily for the past four days and I'm getting into a bit of a rhythm that will help me finish the year strong and start the year even stronger.

Now I don't have all of that pressure during the college football bowl season to be writing down my goals. (And I've gone well into the *NASCAR season before writing down my goals in some

years past...but we won't go there today.)
Take some time this long weekend to do the same. Maybe write them down while you're standing in Black Friday lines or get up early Saturday before the Rivalry Weekend starts or get up early Sunday with a cup of coffee and take some time to review the past year, where you are now, and where you want to be and release the 2019 version of you now.

You'll like what you see. ~*~

*Quick Sidebar: If you like cars and NASCAR you'll like the video with NASCAR champion, Jeff Gordon, in the Pepsi MAX commercial.

It was uploaded to YouTube March 12, 2013, and had nearly 40 million views in a matter of months. That's now a new goal of mine—to get 40 million YouTube views. I wonder how long that will take…?

Sunrise or Sunset? You Get To Decide

Like it or not, December will be here before you know it.

Does this mark the end of a **terrible year** and the beginning of a hopefully-less-terrible year or the end of a terrible year and the beginning of a great year or the end of a great year and the beginning of an even **greater year**?

In the picture below, we cannot tell if the sun is rising or setting, which means we get to **decide** how we want to look at it. We can let the picture speak to us and move us based solely on our own reality and preference.

How you look at your business and your life this time of year is also totally **up to you.**

Sure, you may have endured some great obstacles and even tragedies this past year, but I'm a firm believer that God only gives us what we can handle and that He doesn't call the prepared, **He prepares those He calls.**

Perrito Moreno Glacier, Patagonia, Argentina
May, 2017

Are you thankful for the challenges in your life, which give you opportunities to grow, or are you bitter about them?

In the movie, "**Evan Almighty,**" Morgan Freeman plays God and in the clip below he oh-so eloquently makes this point, as only "God" can. So rather than paraphrase it I'll simply encourage you to take a minute 51 seconds to watch the clip then take another minute or two to think about how that applies to your life. (If you don't get a little teary-eyed at the clip...watch it again with no distractions.)

Neither tough times nor **glorious times** last. **Storms** are always followed by **rainbows**, and clear skies are always followed by storms. Enjoy the "weather" of life. Regardless the circumstances in which you find yourself today, if your focus is clear and you are committed to your goals, you will emerge victorious.

2013 years ago, three wise men followed a star to guide them on their journey to discover a **newborn king.** Christopher Columbus followed the stars to find America. NASA uses the same stars to explore planets, moons and even other solar systems and galaxies.

The exact same stars have been used for thousands of years to help mankind reach their goals. Stars are interesting, are they not?

As Roy Williams pointed out in this week's Monday Morning Memo, the word **start** has the word **star** as its root. Without a solid, stationary reference on which to focus, you can never start with confidence. (And failure to launch is the #1 cause of business failures.)

With a solid focal point to guide you, kings, new worlds, riches and even new galaxies await your discovery. What are you focused on? Is it helping you get to where you want to go? ~✱~

Enjoy the "Pray For The Opportunity" clip mentioned above:
https://www.youtube.com/watch?v=Ikes4yPulmI

Do You Really Want To Live Your Dream?

Do you really want to live your dream?

Sounds like a silly question, doesn't it?

Most people stopped dreaming around **the 4th grade.** Those that were able to either continue dreaming or gave themselves permission to dream again, either think they have to trudge along slowly and methodically to get there <u>waaaaay</u> off into the far distant future, or they don't believe they'll really come true.

So they sit there...collecting dust...mocking us...tormenting us...bringing us down.

"WTH, WES! MY DREAMS THAT ARE SUPPOSED TO MOTIVATE AND INSPIRE ME ARE BRINGING ME DOWN?! HOW MUCH HAPPY EGG NOG HAVE YOU BEEN DRINKING?"

It's sad but true.

See the Golden Gate Bridge above? It gives travelers the ability to walk, bike or motor from San Francisco to Marin County. You can also take a ferry or swim or fly your own helicopter to get between those two points.

Any of those modes of transportation will get you where you want to go. Some in more style and comfort. Some faster than others. Some less expensive than others. Some will create a better story and experience than others. But they'll all get you there, as long as you dream of the journey then START in the right direction on the journey.

"A journey of a thousand miles begins with a single step." Lao-tzu, Chinese philosopher (604 BC - 531 BC)

But most people allow the ocean fog to blind them, to keep them from dreaming, to keep them from starting. (San Francisco and Marin County both exist under the Pacific fog. So do your dreams.)

There will always be fog over the bridge, sharks under the bridge, potholes on the bridge, lanes closed on the bridge, and even accidents on the bridge that shut it down - temporarily.

But if you want to reach your dreams, if the destination is important enough - a sick or injured child, the love of your life, Justin Bieber in concert (aurgh?), your first live interview on national TV, quitting your day job, starting the business of your dreams, taking the vacation of a lifetime with your entire family - are all on the other side of the bridge, the obstacles are worth navigating and enduring and handling.

But keep what they taught us in the Air Force in mind as you begin your journey:
- Don't stand when you can kneel.
- Don't kneel when you can sit.
- Don't sit when you can lie down.
- Don't walk when you can ride.
- Don't ride when you can fly.
- Attack the ambush.

Translated that means:
- Conserve your energy.
- Work smart and efficiently.
- Leverage technology.
- Get where you need to be as fast as you can.
- When the sh*t hits the fan—like it always will—hit back.

It also means **money loves speed**. Take massive action. Our goal in the military is not to "barely" win. Your goal in business is also not to "barely" win.

So pick your destination and start moving towards it now.
Set your New Year's goals now and get started on them, even while you are closing out this year strong.

Seek to get there as quickly as you can, but be willing to endure hardships and struggles and obstacles and detours along the way. ~✲~

Christopher Maloney **wishes he had started 5 years earlier.** Watch the video below to see what I mean. You'll be moved by his story. Hopefully, you'll be so moved you are moved into action to keep his fears from holding you back from your obvious path: **www.youtube.com/watch?v=k1T9-I3wx8I**

8 Years, 18 Months, 8 Hours, 8 Minutes, 8 seconds

To simply look at Big Nick you'd approach him with caution...and half of your friends would actually be **afraid.**

He has a military-style haircut but a **thick beard.**

He's well over six feet tall and about **230 pounds.**

He has **tattoos** from his shins to his torso; from his neck to his arms and down to his knuckles.

He's missing a **tooth.** (You know he's missing a tooth because he's always smiling, but because he's "**big and scary looking**" you only notice the gap instead of the smile.)

What else have you been looking at and **not seeing**? But I digress.

8 Years

For at least **8 years**   Nick has immersed himself into **Brazilian Jiu-Jitsu.**

Unlike the mediocre majority, he's **not a dabbler.**

He's **diligent** in his studies and **methodical** in his efforts.

He's patiently impatient.

The result?

A force of nature who is 100% **martial,** 100% **art,** and 100% **humble.**

18 Months + 8 Hours

For **18 months** I have been studying this martial art for at least **8 hours per week**, including eight of the last 9 days.
That's over **622 hours** of painful, exhausting drills, sparring, and humble pie served hot, fresh, and sweaty.
You'd think that after all that time, effort, and study you'd be pretty good at something, right?

I mean, the average person can read a 250 page book in seven hours so I could've **read 89 books** in this time. If you read 89 books on any subject in 18 months you'd be the leading **authority** in nearly any field in the world.

8 Seconds

But in Brazilian Jiu-Jitsu, after 18 months of training 8 hours per week, you're almost ready to teach an 8-minute class to a **group of 8 year olds.**

I bet you think I'm kidding. Allow me to illustrate.

Despite the amount of effort outlined above, not only Nick, but several other practitioners at my school—some of whom are **65 pounds lighter** than me—can still submit me, i.e. make me cry "UNCLE" in the form of **tapping out**, in as little as **8 seconds.**

EIGHT SECONDS.

Look, getting thrown off a **1,500 pound bull** in under 8 seconds is understandable.

But getting submitted by another human being that quickly? Ugh.

More than once I wanted to say "Pass the Pabst Blue Ribbon and the remote control and turn off the lights when you leave!"

Professor Ricardo Guimaraes, #1 Black Belt Master 5 Lightweight, 2017

(I know "Full Metal Jacket" comes to mind "He's silly and he's ignorant, but he's got guts, and guts is enough." But I digress.)

It's why **so many people quit** Brazilian Jiu-Jitsu—and sales jobs and entrepreneurial ventures: <u>The **struggle** is just too much.</u>

When you fail to find the **easy button** (HINT: It does exist, it's just hard to get to.) you head to the bar and tell anyone who will listen how unlucky you are.

Or you grab the remote and your favorite adult beverage and tell yourself...nothing, **hoping** tomorrow will just magically be better.

However, like the gold in the back of the cave where the **dragon** sleeps, there is an **easy button.**

It's hard to see because it's locked away in the brains of the scary Nicks of the world, who only present it at the end of a hard lesson of **ego-smashing** and a larger helping of humble pie.

(What do you want bad enough to **set aside your ego** and invest time, money, and energy to prepare yourself to recognize, accept, internalize, and apply the lesson the expert gives you?)

8 Minutes

Like a good steak, you have to be **tenderized** in business, in life, and in Brazilian Jiu-Jitsu so you are open and receptive to the lessons of the "easy button" that will make everything you do so much better.

You see after **18 months** of **8 hours** per week of being smashed in **8 seconds** by the guy with **8 years** of experience, he's ready to share—and you're ready to receive—the exact lesson you need that day that will make 1% of what you do **800% better.**

After 18 months **I was struggling** with a particular move and despite hours of practice over the last several months I could not figure out why it was such a problem for me.

In 2.8 seconds   Nick **saw my mistake.**

(It only took him 8 years to be able to see my issue in 2.8 seconds that would've taken me 8 years to see on my own.)

And for **8 minutes** we drilled how to fix that mistake.

And now I **have a plan** for growth that I am excited to implement.

Sure, I need to continue my drills to make this move second-nature, but I know what to do and can **move forward with confidence** now that one more hole in my Brazilian Jiu-Jitsu bucket is patched.

2.8 Seconds or 22 Years?

After **22 years in sales**—12 running my own sales training and marketing consulting business—providing for a family of 9, I'm better at sales than   Nick is at Brazilian Jiu-Jitsu. (If you ask him he'll admit it because we talk sales and marketing often.)

Next week I'll share the **vital concepts** I've learned, applied, and taught to thousands of professional salespeople, sales managers, business owners, and entrepreneurs in 28 countries since 2006.

The entire live, interactive video call will be shorter than an episode of **Game of Thrones**, but a lot more productive.

In 8 seconds you can register at **MakeEverySale.com**.

Now go sell something. ~*~

Nick tried to show us a Native American technique of biting a cactus and getting some kind of stringy-type material out of it…but I'm not 100% sure…but I did get this picture of him doing it. I think he hits golf balls almost as hard as he smashes me on the mats!

It's Good To Be Punched In The Face

Last night I went to my first **MMA fight**.

It was an HOUR from my house...on a 60 degree Sunday night...
(way past my wimpy bedtime)...in a converted garage...with a
dirt parking lot...basically **in a field**...I didn't bring a
jacket...and my **podnuh** (that's Cajun for buddy) had his fight
pushed back **TWO DOGGONE HOURS!**...so I got to watch a lot of
guys get punched in the face.

Which brings me to the picture above.

The dude seated in the cage with his back to us is being tended
to by **EMTs** after he got knocked out in **17 seconds**.

Yep. Seventeen seconds.

(Is it still considered a fight if your opponent doesn't even
have to shower when it's done?)

I've tripped on stairs and taken longer than 17 seconds to fall
down them.

My four year old daughter can hold her breath for 18 seconds.
(We literally just did it at the table to confirm my
suspicion.)

I mean, come on!
Seven-teeny-tiny seconds?

Am I right or am I right, right?
I know what you're thinking.
- "What a wimp!"
- "What a loser!"
- "What a joke!"
- "How embarrassing!"

Now that we have that cleared up, let me ask you something...

When's the last time you put **your pride**, your business, or your physical safety at risk...
...in front of the whole world...
...to find out what you're made of? (With live streaming on Instagram and Facebook these fights were broadcast to the entire world.)

Let me ask you something else...

Would you criticize him to his **face** or would you just think he's a failure as you sip your pumpkin spiced egg nog latte frappuccino with extra cinnamon in your red Starbucks cup while listening to Mariah Carey's **"All I Want For Christmas Is You"** (a full month too soon I might add) as you make new Pinterest boards with your BFFs?

(Lots of keyboard warriors nowadays. I have a trillion dollar idea that would solve that in 30 days, but I digress.)

That guy who got punched in the face and had his fight come to a bloody halt in just 17 seconds **learned more about himself** than you and I did last night and more than most people will learn in 17 years.

Maybe he learned fighting's not his thing.

Maybe he learned he needs to spend more time developing his boxing skills.

But you know what he **learned for sure**?

That he's braver than me and last night he was braver than you.

Why?

Because he stepped barefoot into a cage deep in a California valley hours from home on a cool Sunday night in front of hundreds of people and **faced an opponent** that he did not know armed with nothing more than light gloves, a mouthpiece, and guts.

And he got knocked out in 17 seconds.

As we say in Brazilian Jiu-Jitsu, there are no losses, only victories or learning opportunities.
As we say in **The Make Every Sale Community**, hearing "no" early is a win.

It's much better to hear **NO** within 17 seconds than 17 days, weeks, or months.

It's much better to **hear NO now** so you have time to cultivate another prospect or follow another marketing path than to wine and dine a **lying** prospect who is only **stringing** you along for tickets to the game, expensive Scotch, and to get their current vendor to lower their prices with the quote you give in **desperation** once you realize how much time you've wasted and other opportunities you've lost by hanging on to that "one big deal."

But most of us won't face our biggest fears, risk getting punched in the face, and losing within 17 seconds for all the world to see.

No.

We just "**fake it 'til we make it**" for so long that eventually, the only thing we're making is excuses.

Guess what?

The thing you fear is easier to face—and defeat—when you have a solid team in your corner and a committed team to help you train.

Want a virtual punch in your face to **clear out the head trash**, self-doubt, and negative self-talk you've been using to torture yourself since that **lost sale**, failed venture, divorce, bankruptcy, foreclosure, 3-putt on 18, or being picked last for **kick ball during 4th grade recess**?

Apply for my 90-day private coaching.

It's **reassuringly expensive** and it includes membership in The Make Every Sale Community, so it's the gift to yourself that keeps on giving. (You know that's all you really want for Christmas anyway, so go on. Reward yourself.)
But understand that whether you're in my private consulting or group training, **there is no hiding**. Join if you're ready to endure some short term growing pains, because you will get some digital punches in the nose.

Now go join something.
-Wes

P.S. The picture below is of my friend and Brazilian Jiu-Jitsu training partner, **Squire Redfern**. He's an enrolled member of the **Pala Band of Mission Indians** and at 152 pounds (73 pounds less than me) he tears me up on the mats without breaking a sweat.
Squire didn't make any excuses after losing his first fight last year. He **trained harder** and got back in the cage. The result? **A victory in just 77 seconds**.

And insight into how he can continue to improve.

And the confidence to take on bigger challenges in life, whatever they may be.

Two years ago I wasn't friends with a single Native American...with long braided hair...and tattoos all over their body, who trained to punch people in the nose...now I drove an hour and bought tickets to spend Sunday nights with many of them, and it was an honor.

Whoever said fighting never solved anything was wrong.

I get excited both fighting with and watching Squire Redfern fight, and I know I'm a better man because of it.

P.P.S. This is most of the crew that came to watch **Squire** compete. Rick, Dick, Bryan, me, Carlos, Squire, Anthony, Katie. All fierce **competitors**, committed **practitioners**, and loyal **friends**. **Dick** is 53 and feels like you're fighting rebar.

Bryan once blew out his knee and continued training with little more than duct tape and sticks. **Anthony** is 24 years old and does disco routines on my back, head, and neck despite being a good 50 pounds lighter than me.

Do yourself a favor and find a Brazilian Jiu-Jitsu gym and start training. After two months of extreme soreness... you'll thank me for it.

If you can't afford it, join **The Make Every Sale Community**. I'll show you how to sell more, faster, at higher margin, with less stress, and more fun so you have money to do Brazilian Jiu-Jitsu.

Ever done THIS in an airport restroom?

So I'm standing at the urinal in the Long Beach Airport. (I know. Not exactly "It was the best of times" or "Call me Ishmael" but stick with me.)

Behind me I hear a clanging sound and
"Is anyone in there?"

I assume it's a janitor with a mop but as I finish my business I turn to see a man in his late 60's with a white cane trying to open the **cleaning** closet as he asks boldly...

"Am I getting close to the urinals?"

It was then that I realized what was going on and I told him

"No, sir"
and I began giving him verbal instructions to guid him to the urinals.

But that just seemed weird...and inefficient...and impersonal.

Because he was **struggling** to use his cane and carry his luggage I approached him, placed my hand on his shoulder, and guided him to the first open urinal then turned and walked away.

Humbled...

From maybe a 20 second encounter.

This man had no shame, no frustration, no anger, yet he couldn't easily go to the **restroom** on his own.

Meanwhile we need a day off if our latte doesn't have a smiley face in the foam.

(And don't get me started about the whole *"buy-their-coffee-at-Starbucks-pay-it-forward-to-make-you-feel-better-as-you-post-on-Facebook"* craze. If someone can afford to pay $5 for a $0.95 cup of coffee they're doing just fine. Maybe give that $5 to the next homeless person you see or buy them a cup of coffee or ask the **barista** what the next person's tab is...and give it as a tip to them since they probably can't afford to buy the drinks they make for you. But I digress. **"You do you,"** as the **"woke"** people say. Now where was I?)

The things you and I take for granted are **astonishing**. I'm ashamed at the excuses I've made today, this week, this month, this year, this lifetime.

You should be, too.

You and I have it good, even if we're going through a tough patch, so **put your head down**, peg the pedal to the metal, and get through it.

If you need help putting the pedal to the metal, apply for my 90-day private coaching.

It's reassuringly expensive.

It includes membership in **The Make Every Sale Community,** so you'll get private assistance and semi-private assistance dang-near 24/7.

But only join if you're tired of being **ashamed** of where you are and you're ready to get a little expert guidance for a short, intensive amount of time so you can finally flush your excuses down the drain. (See what I did there?)

Now go flush something.

(Ha. I did it again. Did you notice? You did. I know you did. You know how I know? Because you're smart enough and patient enough to read to this far, and **smart people understand one another,** and we appreciate one another because common sense is so dang un-common. We're like intellectual islands in a sea of muddle-through morons...who seem to want to connect and "get to know" us on **LinkedIn.** But I digress...)

Happy Thanksgiving.

-Wes

P.S. A "**friend**" on Facebook had this to say about my story this week:

"Nice. **However,** in our people with disabilities training we were taught that it is never ok to place your hands on a visually impaired person. Holding them by shoulder is not correct. If they ask for assistance then YOU offer your arm, they place their hand on your arm and you begin to guide them. I think its important for people to know this..."

Talk about a Negative Nellie.

Notice how anything that comes after "**but**" or "**however**"totally negates what came before it?

Don't be that "but-head" with your relatives this week at Thanksgiving...or today online...or Monday at work...or ever for that matter.

And if you do feel compelled to **"teach them a lesson,"** make sure you're 100% right.

You see, Negative Nellie **missed the point** where I explained how that gentleman was struggling with his luggage and his cane so he didn't have a free hand.
And he had already roamed around the restroom for a bit.

And I assumed he wanted to go make **pee-pee-potty** sooner rather than later.

Maybe I could've offered to take his luggage or his cane and lead him with my elbow or shoulder.

Maybe I could've just vectored him in audibly with "You're getting hotter...colder...hotter...hotter... yes! Go ahead and pee-pee!"
Maybe I could've just **ignored** him or pulled out my phone and **recorded** him while mocking him.

Maybe I could've **tripped** him while recording and **mocking**him.
Or I could've just **taken action** and helped the best way I knew how, like I did.

Your **mistakes** are not why you haven't achieved your goals this year...or 2017...or all the way back to 2009. (You know, once the **easy-money went away** in the 2008 collapse?)

It's your distraction **inaction**. It's your **fear** of lie-awake-mistakes. It's your muddled mind cluttered with cliques and click-bait. It's your **information inebriation**, which has lead to your *stuckification.*

It's your wasted time lost on **taking offense** (you're allowed to leave the offense right where it is, ya know? Some of you take offense like it's the last **Cabbage Patch doll** on the shelf on Christmas Eve!) like dear, sweet Negative Nellie, and offering free advice that nobody asked for, fewer people want, and you don't fully understand yourself.

"It's better to keep quiet and have people assume you're an idiot than to open your mouth and remove all doubt."

Succeeding in sales is easy when you know how to succeed in life.

And you can keep your head down and get the scars as you figure it all out on your own, or you can invest in shortening the learning curve by 10 or 20 years.

It's your choice. And choosing to think about it or wait until after **Thanksgiving** or Christmas or the New Year or President's Day or Valentine's Day or St. Patrick's Day or your tax return or **Memorial Day** or Father's Day or Independence Day or Labor Day or Halloween...we'll be right back in November, except we'll both be a year older, and you'll be...?

Show Me Your Tools

My dad has worked in commercial insulation his entire life. He has run some major jobs where he oversaw 600+ workers responsible for both the insulation and scaffolding.

With that many workers he was approached daily by people looking for work who would typically overstate their experience and abilities, to receive higher pay. However, my dad had a foolproof system for gauging just how good they were. All he said was **"show me your tools."**

My brother-in-law is a professional craftsman.When he pulls up to the house you know he's a pro based solely on the tools in the back of his truck, in his tool chest, and on the trailer he tows with additional equipment. He has the right tool for any job. Ditto for Dr. Fernie, our mobile mechanic. Ditto for Juan, my gardener, who runs a tight ship with a professional crew.

When these workers who wanted to work for my dad came back with some knock-off branded, rusty wrapped in newspaper he either told them to take a hike or to accept an entry-level position, because they just proved they were not worth hiring at the highest level.

Just this weekend in one of the CRM groups I belong to on Facebook, a member was asking how to hack his CRM so he could save a whopping $59/mo (and put his entire business—and the security of all of his contacts and customers—at risk.)

He didn't want to pay $59/mo for the E-commerce upgrade for his CRM because he "didn't need it"…but he needed to collect the credit card information of his contacts. (Truth really is stranger than fiction.)

So he was asking how to make landing pages with split fields to collect this information in blocks of 8-digits because if he got all 16 digits in one field his CRM correctly assumed it was a credit card and encrypted the information.

"YEAH, I'M GONNA NEED ME ABOUT A DOZEN ROLLS OF DUCT TAPE, 46 BALL BEARINGS, 127 LINEAR FEET OF CHICKEN WIRE, A WHEELBARROW, A SLEEVE OF COPENHAGEN® TOBACCO, TWO CASES OF BUD LIGHT®, AND A HALF

GALLON OF LIGHTER FLUID. AND BE QUICK ABOUT IT! AND DON'T ASK WHY. I'M WHATCHACALL...A PRO-FESSIONAL!"

I mean, who the heck does this nowadays? I'll tell you who. We all do to one degree or another. It's smart to be frugal and to look for cheap or free ways to get the job done, but only to a point. Then it's silly—and in this guy's case—risky. Like lawsuit-ruin-your-life risky.

When it comes to both tools and consulting/coaching/mentoring this is the adage I recommend you live and grow by:

It's better to pay more than you wanted than less than you should.

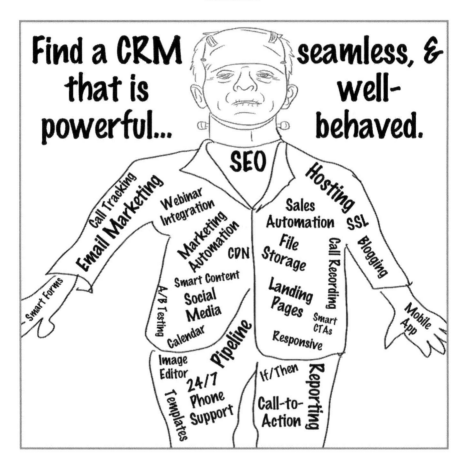

Visit BestCRMForMe.com To Find Yours

Trust me on this.

Back in 2008, when I was still a one-man show with no website, no merchant account, no office, and no staff I jumped into Infusionsoft with little more than inspiration and the willingness to apply ample perspiration until I got where I needed to go.

Back then it was $5,000 down and $299/mo. For that price you got a worthless onboarding experience, a PDF, a hard-to-use but powerful small business sales and marketing automation software platform, a 5-user license (for me and four imaginary friends), unlimited phone support (as long as you called during business hours Monday-Friday), and a handful of decent tools and examples to help you automate, integrate, and dominate your niche.

This software was sold as "all-in-one," which was a convenient half-truth that angered me on a monthly if not daily basis for years because I regularly ran into situations that were not met with their software. So I had to live without that functionality, do it myself, hire someone to do it, or buy additional software and hope I could get it to play nicely with Infusionsoft.

Before long I felt like Dr. Frankenstein stealing and stitching together various body parts hoping to create a living creature that would do as I said.

Then I remembered my own advice and invested in the tools I needed to get the job done.

I applied my own **Process Before Login** to myself—and available to you for free at **www.TheSalesWhisperer.com/pbl**. Once I documented my current and/or ideal process I found the right tool for the job.

Yes, my expenses increased but my frustration decreased as my income and free time went up. Now a large portion of my income comes from helping people find and apply the right tool for the jobs they need.

That's why I created the **BestCRMForMe.com** custom survey. It asks you the real questions you must address so. you, too, can find the right tool for the job.

Now it's my #1 lead-generator and has been for years. Follow that link to see how I made my misery my ministry, and how you can, too. ~✱~

Resources

The CRM Butler Is Here For You

Get affordable, expert, timely help to automate, integrate, and dominate your sales. Delight is now being served.

- Get unlimited support for your CRM, shopping cart, marketing automation platform, third party plugins, and more with our unique offering at **TheCRMButler.com**.
- Grow Your Sales Sales With Hundreds of Free Interviews on The Sales Podcast: **www.TheSalesPodcast.com**
- Join The Conversation and Engage With Other Sales Professionals For Free: **www.TheImplementors.com**
- Join My Most-Affordable Sales Training With 41 Videos, 70+ Page Workbook, Live Weekly Calls, Private Group, Templates, Timely Support, and More In Make Every Sale: **www.MakeEverySale.com**
- Find The Technology Tools You Need To Automate, Integrate, and Dominate on The CRM Sushi Podcast: **www.CRMSushi.com**
- Hire Great Sales People With The Affordable No More Sales Duds Program: **www.NoMoreSalesDuds.com**
- Find The Best CRM For You: **www.BestCRMForMe.com**
- Order "The Definitive Guide To Infusionsoft" Book: **www.BestCRMBook.com**

- Get Non-Cheesy, Non-Sales, Timely Tools, Tips, and Tactics To Grow Your Sales With The Weekly Whisper: **www.WeeklyWhisper.com**
- Your 3 Frogs, New Year's Gift: **www.TheSalesWhisperer.com/tgr**
- Control Every Sale With The Sales Agenda: **www.TheSalesAgenda.com**
- Get 21 Years of The Best Sales Secrets In Just 21 Pages For Free: **www.TheBestSalesSecrets.com**

About the Author

Wes Schaeffer is an author, speaker, trainer and consultant in Southern California. He is known as "The Sales Whisperer®" and is the world's leading consultant on incorporating key sales and marketing fundamentals to grow with marketing automation software and CRMs. Clients and CRM users who follow his methods generate over $500,000,000 in sales annually.

He consults with companies of all sizes—from solo-preneurs to members of the Fortune 50—running both online and traditional brick-and-mortar businesses.

Prior to his consulting career, Wes worked in the financial services industry, retail, real estate and high tech. He successfully sold across the kitchen table in the Deep South and also sold to Google, in the heart of Silicon Valley.

A graduate of both the United States Air Force Academy and Texas A&M, Wes likes to say he is bi-lingual in "Geek" and "Bubba," and he is fluent in both. Like the trail-blazing direct marketers Claude Hopkins and Perry Marshall, Wes has an engineering background and a penchant for writing persuasive copy. He has published hundreds of posts and articles on sales, copywriting, marketing and Infusionsoft.

He loves delivering keynote speeches around the world and has trained sales people, sales managers, franchise owners, entrepreneurs and business owners in over 100 industries.

Please connect with Wes wherever you hangout online:
  LinkedIn: www.linkedin.com/in/thesaleswhisperer/
  Facebook: www.facebook.com/thesaleswhisperer
  Twitter: twitter.com/saleswhisperer
  YouTube: www.youtube.com/saleswhisperer
  Instagram: instagram.com/saleswhisperer
  Email: www.thesaleswhisperer.com/contact/

.₌ₛ$$$$$$$$$$$$$$$$$$$ₛₛ.

Notes

Made in the USA
Middletown, DE
21 April 2019